GLOBALIZATION AND THE CHANGING SCENARIO OF CULTURAL INTERACTION (Manipur Experience)

GLOBALIZATION AND THE CHANGING SCENARIO OF CULTURAL INTERACTION

(Manipur Experience)

Edited by

Prof. N. Joykumar Singh

Centre for Manipur Studies
Manipur University, Imphal
&
AKANSHA PUBLISHING HOUSE
NEW DELHI-110 002 (INDIA)

AKANSHA PUBLISHING HOUSE
4649/21B, Ansari Road
Darya Ganj
New Delhi - 110 002
Ph. : 23263193 / 9811582579
Email: ektabooks@yahoo.com

Globalization and the Changing Scenario of Cultural Interaction (Manipur Experience)

First Edition 2007
ISBN 81-8370-085-3

[The responsibility for the facts stated, conclusions reached etc., is entirely that of the Author(s). The publisher bears no responsibility for them, whatsoever.]

PRINTED IN INDIA

Published by M.P. Misra for Akansha Publishing House, New Delhi and Printed at Aryan Enterprises, Delhi.

Preface

Manipur has been experiencing various forms of cultural interactions since early historic times. Streams of migrants came to this state during different phases of history. The state, thus, has experienced the assimilation and acculturation of the people of South Asia, Central Asia, Eastern Asia, South-East Asia in general and the Aryan culture, the Tai culture and the Mongoloid culture in particular. Many religions viz., Hinduism, Buddhism, Islam and Christianity transformed the social and religious practices of the state in remarkable way. At the same time the emerging socio-cultural elements were also transformed to adapt to the earlier socio-cultural environment of the state like traditional animism, heliocentric and different tribal cults.

During the post-Independence period, the cultural interactions took a new turn. Development incentives viz., establishment of industries, commercialization of agriculture, expansion in transport and communication, etc., transformed the economy, polity, society and even the demographic composition of the state. Entrepreneurs, corporates, businessmen, laborers and even refugees migrated into the state in large number thereby resulting in a change in the demographic composition of the state. However, the economy of the state remained more or less backward and agrarian, with consumer items and other modern amenities of life coming from other developed areas.

Against this backdrop the indigenous people, who have lost their part tradition, resort to measures to assert their own identities: economic and political identities in general and cultural identity in particular. These measures took many forms e.g., armed struggles, ethnic and communal conflicts and even the 'Cultural war' against the 'alien' cultures. This development is particularly evident in Manipur. It is at this juncture that, the impact of globalization produces new forms of cultural interactions in the state. These new cultural interactions which is mainly through the media, both print and electronic, erode the traditional values, ethos and practices.

Since, the early '90s the forms of cultural interactions arising out of the new world order have been addressed substantially and extensively. However, the unique form of cultural interactions experienced in Manipur in the backdrop of armed conflicts, ethnic conflicts, demographic transformation and even globalization is still grossly neglected. It was in this perspective that Centre for Manipur Studies, Manipur University, Imphal organized a national seminar on the theme "Globalization and Changing Scenario of Cultural Interaction: Manipur Experience" with the objective of addressing the neglected theme of cultural interactions in the context of globalization in Manipur. The present volume is an outcome of its proceeding papers contributed by the established scholars and young researchers who are currently engaged in the study of the themes and topics which are addressed in the Seminar. It includes the traditional cultural values of Manipur, Colonial impact on cultural values, Religious movements and cultural synthesis, and gobalization and cultural interactions in Manipur.

Dr. Lokendra Arambam in his paper, "Globalization and Cultural Encounters: The Manipuri Perspective", highlights the process of globalisation as experienced in other parts of the world including India. He argues that Manipur has yet to grasp the implications and ramifications and the various political and cultural movements as responses to the new global force are analytically examined. Further a textual analysis of India's 'Look East Policy' is analyzed vis-a-vis the social, cultural, political and economic environment of Manipur.

In the paper entitled "New Dimensions and Challenges for Human Rights in the Globalization: Cultural Relativism and Commodification" Dhanabir Laishram makes a critical observation of cultural relativism as an associated element of globalisation. He put forward the argument that cultural relativism has led to the confusion of nationalism and in many ways the former becomes synonymous with cultural assimilation. The reality of globalisation for all the third and fourth world country was that the common culture engendered in the process of globalisation was based on economic basis which is advantageous to the first world countries. He argues that the new global order as responsible for the myriad of problems faced by the people in the North-Eastern Region of India. He concluded that unless there is check in the form of cultural relativism and cultural commodification superimposed by the first world countries and their local collaborators, the dream of another world is impossible.

Professor Amar Yumnam's paper "Globalisation, Culture and Development", highlights a brief history of globalisation since the Roman Era. Further, he emphasizs the necessity of hegemony as the major leading character of each epoch of globalisation giving its impact in all spheres of life. It shows the relationship between cultural and developmental economics in every era of globalisation.

P. Milan in his paper "Globalisation, Monoculturalism and Ethnicity" raises a polemic against single line pressure of cultural pattern from above with negative impact due to Globalisation that also attacks all the ethnic values. Aheibam Koering's paper "Colonialism, Culturocide and Denial of Shares History: An Experience in Manipur Hills" contends that the conversion to Christianity in its introductory phase was detached from the value-free neutrality as it was done under the patronage of the colonizers. The paper also highlights the negative impact on the indigenous peoples of the Manipur hills when their existing ways of thinking were encountered with the emerging ways of thinking brought about by Christianity and also explores the contemporary social crisis of Manipur in the form of fragmentation and the rise of micro nationalism as a consequent fallout of the concomitant deficit policy in their history, which engendered the denial of shares history. He argues that ethnicity and identity assertion in the form of ethnic violence can be reconciled by reappraising their close affinities and socio-cultural ties with each other.

Dr. Vijaylakshmi's paper entitled "Religious Movements and Cultural Synthesis in Manipur: An Observation on Manipuri Hinduism" focuses on the origin of the Meitei belief system and the cultural interaction with other places, viz., China, Burma (Myanmar), the Ahom Kingdom of Assam, etc. She puts an emphasis on the impact of cultural and religious practices on that of Manipur through the ages. Syed Ahmad's paper entitled 'Regional formulation of Islam in Manipur' is an attempt to analyse the cultural accretions and influences from the local socio-cultural environment on the Muslims of Manipur. Various practices that were adopted by the Muslims to acclimatize themselves with the local environment and later on the practices to cleanse the non-Islamic accretions are also analyzed in his paper. M. Bobo's paper "Globalisation and Culture: Manipur Experience" makes an attempt to define Globalisation with illustrations in the first place and gives examples and impact of Globalisation on the poor countries in comparison with rich countries with data from United Nations Development Programme (UNDP) and World Bank. Jagat Thoudam's paper "Globalisation and Cultural Interactions in Manipur", highlighted the individualistic pattern in all works of life and culture with Globalisation thereby affecting collectivism which is a part of tradition.

Professor W. Nabakumar's paper "Cultural Interaction and Growth: A Case Study of Leimaram, a Scheduled Caste of Manipur" analyses the little tradition of Leimaram people adopting the great tradition of the Hindus thereby indicating the metamorphic questions were raised for clarifications on the conceptualization of great and little traditions. The paper entitled "Globalisation and Krishna Consciousness: An Overview" by Amal Sanasam analyses the movement of ISKCON in Manipur valley. The writer argues that the 'Krishna Consciousness Movement' is the first concept of globalising the Indian culture in modern times. The impact of Vaishnavism cult on religion and culture of Manipur is analyzed in the presentation. The adjustment of the Vaishnavism to the local conditions and the effort of ISKCON, Manipur towards evolving a peace process are also discussed. In his paper "Place in a Placeless World: Nationalism and Globalisation in Manipur", Konjengbam Meghachandra Singh makes an attempt to analyse some aspects of nationalism in the age of globalisation in Manipur context. His argument is that globalisation refers to time-space compression and thus the significance of 'place' has been reduced with the expansion of 'global village'. However many parts of the world are experiencing various political movements at national and sub-national levels, asserting territory and identity. These national and sub-national movements in Manipur face a number of obstacles viz., inter-outfit conflict and clash, factional rivalry and cultural imperialism, the last of which is patronized by globalisation itself. On the other hand, globalisation itself is almost an unrestrained phenomenon. The writer raises a question as to whether globalisation will take over nationalism and sub-nationalism.

I, on behalf of the Centre for Manipur Studies (CMS), Manipur University express my sincere gratitude to Prof. N. Bijoy, Former Vice-Chancellor of Manipur University for his generous initiative organizing the seminar. I also extend my sincere thanks and gratitude to the present Vice-Chancellor of the University for showing keen interest and also for his generous initiative in the publication of the proceeding papers. The seminar achieved success because of the valuable papers of the contributors as well as the contributions made by the staff of the Centre and the office of the Dean of School of Social Sciences of the University. Their contributions right from organizing the Seminar till the finalisation of this book are also duly acknowledged and deserve appreciation. I also express my indebtedness to Shri M.P. Misra, Akansha Publishing House, New Delhi for readily accepting to co-publish this book with the Centre.

PROF. N. JOYKUMAR SINGH
Director
Centre for Manipur Studies
Manipur University

List of Contributors

Ahmed, Syed, Freelance Researcher.

Arambam, Lokendra, Former Director, Visual Research Centre (AVRC), Manipur University and Theatre Personality.

Brara, N. Vijayalakshmi, Freelance Researcher.

Khangamcha, P. Milan, Assistant Professor, Department of Philosophy, Manipur University.

Konjengbam Mehachandra, Ph.D. Student, Department of History, Manipur University.

Laishram, Dhanabir, Guest Faculty, Department of Political Science, Manipur University.

Maisnam, Chinglen, Assistant Professor, Department of Economics, Manipur University.

Nabakumar, W., Professor, Department of Anthropology, Manipur University.

Sanasam, Amal, Research Associate, Centre for Manipur Studies, Manipur University.

Singh, Aheibam Koireng, Research Associate, Centre for Manipur Studies, Manipur University.

Thoudam, Jagat, Social Activist and Social Observer.

Yumnam, Amar, Professor, Department of Economics, Manipur University.

Contents

1

Globalisation, Culture and Development: An Economist's Perspective

—AMAR YUMNAM

Introduction

Globalisation is the most tantalizing term in the world political economy today, and to come it even causes titillation. The sweep of this as both a term and a phenomenon is such that even anti-globalisation is now a globalized network.

But what then in globalisation? As Karlsson says it "refers to a number of inter-related economic, technological, social, political and cultural changes that together have so intensified interdependence that anyone who wants to exercise control over her future must do so with others locally, nationally, and globally" (Karlsson, 2001, p 8). In other words, globalization is an on going process of global integration that encompasses: (i) economic integration through trade, investment and capital flows; (ii) political interactions, (iii) information and information technology, and (iv) culture." (Panayoton, 2000, p. 1). Globalisation, as economists perceive it, covers easing of transborder movement of goods and services, foreign direct investment, financial capital and migration (Williamson, 1999; O'Rourke, 2002).

Through the intense debate on the subject is relatively recent, the phenomenon is definitely not a new one. Speaking of around A.D. 150 Brown writes,

> ". . . it was possible for a young student, Tatian, to pass from the eastern, Syrian, fringe of the Roman empire to Rome, speaking Greek philosophical culture. . . . To humbler men, [the Roman Empire] meant wider horizons and unprecedented opportunities for travel; it meant the erosion of local differences through trade and emigration; and the weakening of ancient barriers before new wealth and new criteria of status" (Brown, 1971, p. 60). This was in a time nearly two thousand years before an English princess with her Egyptian boyfriend crashes in a French tunnel, riding a German car with Dutch engine and driven by a Belgian drunk on Scottish whisky, followed closely by Italian paparazzi on a Japanese bike, treated by an American doctor using Brazilian medicine. (I am paraphrasing an SMS created by an Indian using a Chinese mobile smuggled by a Pakistani through a Nepali courier). In the case of Manipur, a contemporary researcher writes: "To prove that Manipur lies in the cultural area of South-east Asia with cultural layers of East Asia and other regions, e.g., a south Asian tint on it, will not be a difficult task" (Tomba, 2005, p. 21).

What I am basically trying to say is that globalisation as a process is as old as human civilization though the scale and geographical coverage might differ due to the differing levels of development—transportation, communication and information technology.

Conventional Logic

I understand that the conventional rationals of the economists legitimizing globalisation might be of little interest to the wider audience here, but kindly allow me to briefly mention the factors of consideration. Globalisation, as defined earlier, is understood to

(a) enhance efficiency of allocation of resources both nationally and globally, and thus raising the growth rate. The rising growth rate further leads to reduction of poverty;

(b) intensify competition among nation states, and in the process contributes to enhanced governmental accountability. In other words, the credibility of governments is increased both nationally and globally; and

(c) facilitate flow of technology.

I will, however, not dwell long on the economic logic, but rather concentrate on the empirics and the debates surrounding them. (Those interested in theory may refer to, among others, Aghion's paper in Aghion and Williamson, 1998).

Globalisation Epochs

As far as I understand, we are yet to have a periodisation approach from the angle of the Orientals. I am not aware of periodisation approaches using Hindu civilization or Buddhist culture as the basis. So I shall, by necessity, confine my periodisation approach to the lines already adopted in the globalisation literature, which is fundamentally based on Occidental civilization.

As implied in the quotation from Brown's work in the beginning of this paper, we may think of the Roman Empire as the first period of globalisation. This period covering two to three centuries extended over the land area from the Euphrates to Scotland and from the Gibraltar to Armenia. However, due to reasons of availability and reliability of data, most of the globalisation studies confine to the two recent epochs, one extending from about the mid-19th century to 1914 and another from post-World War II (1950) to till date. In keeping with this tradition, my discussion here shall confine to these two periods, 1850-1914 and 1980-2005 (some confine the 1850-1914 period to 1870-1939. Estevadeordal *et al.*, 2002). My selection of 1980 rather than 1950 as the initial year for contemporary globalisation is because of China and India factors and the end of cold war.

Driving Forces

The first modern globalisation epoch (1850-1914) was preceded by dismantling of mercantilism and adoption of liberal trade policy, recovery after the Napoleonic Wars, structural transformation consequent upon agricultural depression in England and sharp drop in transport costs. (Lindert and Williamson, 2001). To these forces, a new dimension has also been added in a well researched paper by Estevadeordal and others - the common currency effect (Estevadeordal *et al.*, 2002). During the period from about 1800 to 1914, international trade volumes rose by a factor of about twenty and about ten relative to world output.

The current globalisation process is driven by the following factors (Agosin and Tussie, 1992):

1. Emergence of foreign direct investment as a more significant factor than domestic capital formation and rise in the volume of intra-industry trade globally;
2. The growing " internationalization of finance" and the accompanying massive increase in global financial transactions;
3. The communication revolution intensifying and altering the traditional comparative advantage positions (see also Evans and Harrigan, 2003);
4. The emergence of information technology as a general purpose technology contributing to internationalizing of both information and technology.

Hegemon and Imperialism

While accepting the above driving forces as significant factors in the globalisation process, there is now an intense debate as to whether these were enough to explain the phenomenon. One view is that, given the necessity of safe transportation and communication for a sustained growth of production and exchange, globalization can occur only under the aegis of a hegemon. The first globalisation could occur because of the duration and penetration of the Roman empire; Roman imperialism ensured the first globalisation. The globalisation of the mid-19th to early 20th century could take place under the British imperialism, and ended when fiercely challenged by Germany. The end of the cold war and the emergence of a unipolar world has made globalisation under a new hegemon a possibility once again.

While the relationship between imperialism and globalisation is more or less an accepted one, it is the impact which is being debated. While the de-industrialisation in India under the British rule is a strong thesis here, Western economists are working overtime to refute the negative impact of globalisation under imperialism: "Given the structural constraints imposed by location, climate and geography, on the way that the world economy evolved, as well as the entrenched positions of privilege, Europeans had already acquired, from centuries of successful mercantilism, comparisons between the colonized and autonomous economies of the Third World does not, however, leave an impression that any potential or counterfactual gap in transactions costs could have been wide enough to proclaim that the continued divergence in standards of living between the west and the Rest could be strongly linked to the persistence of imperialism between 1815 and 1948" (O'Brien, 2004, p. 50) reflecting the opposite view on Prakash writes:

> "Given the reasonably resilient internal dynamics of the Indian economy, the colonial period was not altogether devoid of all growth though one could legitimately take the position that almost certainly things would have been distinctly better if the colonial episode had never happened". (Prakash, 2004, p. 40).

Globalisation and Convergence

Whatever the driving force behind the different globalisation epochs, what is of concern to us is its impact. Has the globalisation led to reduction in within country and across the country inequalities? Has it induced faster growth? Has it had any positive effect on poverty reduction? I shall now turn to the studies relating to these.

It has been found that the declines in transport costs between 1840 and 1910 was much more dramatic than in the post-1945 period; in fact, ocean freight rates have increased in the sort 1945 period, though there has been a decline in the air-freights (Harley, 1988; Hummels, 1999). So global integration in commodity markets was much greater in the 19th century than in the late 20th century (O'Rourke, 2002; Estevadeordal *et al.*, 2002).

As regards foreign direct investment, it is more diversified and more growth enhance today than in the 19th century (O'Rourke, 2002).

Regarding migration, we can definitely say that the 19th century. The migration from the Europe to the New World in the 19th century was of the order like 60 million individuals (Lindert and Williamson, 2001, p. 16) whereas firm data are not available on the south-south movements. The 19th century movement involved mainly poorer people moving to richer countries and hence was equality enhancing. But, thanks to the various restricts on migration in the 20th century involving selection bias, the movement of people now is not equality enhancing both globally and nationally.

The gap in per capita share of GDP between Western Europe (richest region) and Africa (poorest region) was around three to one about a century and a half ago (Maddison, 1995). Today the per capita income gap between Switzerland and Mozambique is a hopping 400 to 1. It is as if "divergence, big time" (Pritchett, 1997).

Lindert and Williamson (2001) argue that the British-led globalisation was unambiguously egalitarian at both the national and global level, "while the American liberalization in the 20th century was not". A recent study by Dollar and Kray (2001) speaks of the growth and poverty and poverty reduction implications of trade liberalization. However, this has not one without challenge. There are equally strong arguments refuting the benefits of financial integration to the developing countries (Gourinchas, 2004). Pissaarides (1997) and Wood (1997) reach at completely contradictory results of the welfare benefits of globalisation. Rodrik (2000) and Rodriguez and Rodrik (1999) refute the very growth enhancing effects of trade and argue that globalisation can never be a substitute for a development strategy.

Culture and Globalisation

The interface of culture, globalisation and growth is a relatively new area of research and the results are still highly tentative. (McCleary and Barro, 2003; Burro and McCleary 2003; Lal, 1999). In particular the interaction between culture and growth in a context of globalisation is yet to invaded by the economists though directions are now clearly visible.

The Road Ahead

While globalisation by itself may or may not deliver, the institutional requirements are highly demanding (Rodrik 2000). These would have far reaching effects on culture and governance in any country going for globalisation. Further as globalisation continues, the growth requirements for a given goal has been found to be rising in every period. Further, the role of geographical variables (case of access to market and input sources) in two harvesting of benefits for globalisation is an area yet to be properly explored.

Above all, globalisation in the past has always had it backlash. The association of the current globalisation, as in the past, with a hegemon will itself make it impalatable to the large masses of people.

REFERENCES

Aghion, Philipp and Jeffrey G. Williamson, (1998), *Growth, Inequality and Globalisation: Theory, History, and Policy*, Cambridge University Press, Cambridge.

Agosin, Manuel R. and Diana Tussie (1992), "Globalisation, regionalisation and new dilemmas in trade policy for development", *World Competition*, 15: 37-63.

Barro, Robert J. and Rachel M. McCleary (2003), *Religion and Economic Growth*, Harvard University, mimeo.

Blattman, Christopher and Jeffrey G. Williamson (2004), The Importance of the terms of trade on Economic Development in the Periphery, 1870-1939: Volatility and Secular Change, Harvard Institute of Economic Research, *Dissension Paper No. 2040*, July.

Brown, Peter (1971), *The World of Late Antiquity AD 150-750*, W.W. Norton, New York and London.

Crafts, Nicholas (2000) *Globalisation and Growth in the 20th Century*, International Monetary Fund, Working Paper No. 44.

Dollar, David and Aart Kray (2001), *Trade, Growth, and Poverty*, Development Research Group, World Bank.

Easterly, W. M. Kremer, L. Pritchett and L. H. Summers (1993) "Good policy or good luck? Country growth performance and temporary shocks", *Journal of Monetary Economics*, 32: 459-83 (fundamental determinants of growth-more persistent than the growth rate the try to explains.

Estevadeordal, Antoni, Brian Franty and Alan M. Taylor (2002), The Rise and Fall of World Trade, 1870-1939, National Bureau of Economic Research, Working Paper No. 9318.

Evans, Carolyn L. and James Harrigan (2003) *Distance, Time, and Specialization*, National Bureau of Economic Research, Working Paper No. 9729.

Faria, Joao Ricardo, and Mignel Leon-ledesma (2004), *A Cultural Heritage and Growth*, University of Texas, Dallas, mimeo.

Gourinchas, Pierre-Olivier and Olivier Jeanne (2004), *The Elusive Gains from International Financial Integration*, International Monetary Fund, Working Paper.

Harley, C. Knick (1988), "Ocean freight rates and productivity, 1740-1913: the primacy of mechanical invention reaffirmed", *Journal of Economic History*, 48: 851-76

Hummels, David (1999), The wealth and poorly of Nations: Why some are so Rich and some so Poor.

Karlsson, Mats (2001) "Opening Address" at the Annual World Bank Conference on Development Economics, ABCDE 2000, World Bank, pp. 7-11.

Lal, Deepak (1999), *Unintended Consequences: The Impact of Factor Endowments, Culture and Politics on Long run Economic Performance*, OUP, New Delhi.

Lindert, Peter H. and Jeffrey G. Williamson, (2001) *Globalisation and Inequality: A long History*, Invited Lecture, ABCDE-Europe, Barcelona.

Maddison, Aungus (1995), Monitoring the World Economy, 1820-1992, OECD, Paris.

McCleary, Rachel M. and Robert J.Barro (2003), Religion and Political Economy in an International Panel, Harvard University, mimeo.

O'Brien, Patrick Karl (2004), Colonies in a Globalizing Economy 1815-1948, Department of Economic History, London School of Economics, *Working Paper No.08/04*, mimeo.

O'Rourke, Kevin H. (2002) "Globalisation and inequality: historical trends", *Annual World Bank Conference on Development Economics 2001/2002*, World, pp 39-67. Dollar, David (1999), "On the threshold of the Third Globalisation: why liberal capitalism might fail?", Research Department, World Bank, Mimeo.

Panayoton, Theodore (2000), Globalisation and Environment, Background Paper, Human Development Report 1999, Centre for International Development, Harvard University.

Pissarides, Christopher A (1997), "Learning by trading and the returns to human capital in developing countries", *World Bank Economic Review*, 11: 19-32

Prakash, Om (2003), The transformation from a pre-colonial to a colonial order: The case of India, mimeo.

Pritchett, L. (1997), "Divergence, big time", *Journal of Economic Perspectives*, 11: 3-17.

Rao, A consumption affordability index.

Rodrignez, Francisco and Dani Rodrik (1999), Trade Policy and Economic Growth: A skeptic's guide to the Cross-National Literature, National Bureau of Economic Research, Working Paper No. 7081.

Rodrik, Dani (2000), "Can integration into the world economy substitute for a development strategy?", ABCDE-Europe Conference, Paris.

Tomba, T (2005) *East and South-east Asia - Folklore and Cultural Affinity with Manipur Studies*, Manipur University.

Wood, Adrian (1997), "Openness and wage inequality in developing countries: the Latin American Challenge to East Asian Conventional Wisdom", *World Bank Economic Review*, 11: 33-57.

Yurndorfer, Harriet T. (2004), *Imperialiasm, Globalisation, and Pustic Finance: The case of late Qing China*, University of Leiden, mimeo.

2

New Dimensions and Challenges for Human Rights in the Globalisation (Cultural Relativism and Cultural Commodification)

—DHANABIR LAISHRAM

Basically human right activists are bepeppering against the state terrorism like killing, torturing, rape, disappearance, custodial death and detention because for human right abuses and crimes done by non state actors, we have police and law courts. Besides, another burden is kept on their heads again to protect the rights of the people which is being violated by the globalisation. Fidel Castro rightly remarked, "I did'nt oppose the globalisation". That means the open discourse is the victims should become the killers because of inability to pass out the frozen layers of exploitation and oppression in the uncountable numbers of global villages. So we have to analyse the associated elements of globalisation mainly cultural relativism and confusion of nationalism. Here one comes to understand new human rights dimensions and its obstacle and challenges. Even it could associate the process of cultural assimilation and confusion of nationalism.

Globalisation: Conceptual and Historical Analysis

In the post-cold war period, one could witness a unipolar system in the international politics after the disintegration of the USSR and their reversion to capitalism along with the East European countries. The most dominant economic campaign in this period (1990s) was 'globalisation'. The description of globalisation is the widening and deepening of international glows of trade, finance and information in a single integrated global market whereas the prescription for this was to liberalize national and global markets. The prescription cannot be administered at will on the sovereign states by force of arms as in 19th or early 20th century. Therefore, the process of globalisation has been manoeuvered in a clever and subtle way though it is associated with the sanction and plundering that were experienced in the colonialism of the 19th and 20th centuries. For doing so, the governments of the states should be agreeable to changes necessary and therefore a well thought-out logic, namely "Economic Reforms" was formulated. These reforms are mainly liberalization of national market and free entry of the multinationals, privatization of economic power. For these reforms to be undertaken there should be flexible structure of administration and governance for which there should be the Structural Adjustment Programme (SAP). If all these go well in the less-developed and developing countries, the highly industrialized countries can control all the economic, social and cultural activities of the poorer nations and the poor people of all the nations with impurity and conviction. Such is the design of globalisation[1]. Besides, the question of culture commodification could not also be discarded because it plays important role to save causing of economic tsunami of first world countries. So that the advanced countries tried to Universal Declaration of Human Rights.

Here, one could react and has reasonable claims to attain their best setters. But the problems are that in case of human right, it could be universal. So we the people of world always accepted and quailed the universal declaration of human rights and its articles. The same could not be conceived in the minds of second, third and fourth world peoples regarding universalist of cultural relativism. To them cultural relativism regarding human rights and democracy is self-defeating parochial and just plain wrong.

Universalising of Human Rights versus Cultural Relativism

In the present discourse concerning human rights, cultural relativism is presented as a main challenge to their universality.

As observed by Brezezinski (1995):

> "Culture is now going to be the dividing line in the debate over the question of freedom and the question of human rights. We are all familiar with the cultural argument. It rejects the notion of inalienable human rights on the ground that this notion merely reflects a very provincial, western perspective."[2]

The acceptance of the very idea that person belonging to one culture should not judge the policies and values of other cultures, that any system of common values cannot and does not exist. Indeed, it undermines the very basis of the international community and the human family. They cannot function without the existence of standard allowing them to judge what is right or wrong, what is good or bad.[3] The world commission on culture and development in its report "Our Creative Diversity", pointed out that the logical and ethical difficulty about relativism is that it must also endorse absolutism and dogmatism. Cognitive relativism is nonsense, moral relativism is tragic.[4]

Cultural relativism in its extreme interpretations may even lead to or justify theories like that on conflict of civilization put forward by S. Huntington. In his opinion, the globalisation of the modern world has given rise to a conflict between the basic cultural systems. The theory of the beginning of an age of irreconcilable battles between the most powerful civilizations does not correspond to reality. Cultural diversity and plurality of cultures have to be seen as positive factors leading to inter-cultural dialogue. In the modern world, cultures are not isolated. They interact peacefully and influence each other. The inter-cultural dynamics is set in motion by the contemporary processes of globalisation which lead, not without tension, to the emergence, consolidation or reformulation of specific cultural and ethical values common to the various cultural areas.[5] Any culture in relation to and comparison with other cultures may find its own idiosyncrasies and peculiarities, its strong and its weak points.

The Vienna Conference and Rejection of Cultural Relativism

The analysis of statements during the Vienna Conference shows that the universality of human rights was not openly challenged, whereas cultural specificity were seen by many states as being fully compatible notions. The delegates from Tunisia, Kuwait, Iran, Vietnam, Etyma, Netherlands, Costa Rica and Bangladesh, recognizing the universal values of human rights, then stressed on cultures of humanity. However, no ready-made model can be presented at the universal level since the historical and cultural realities of each nation and the traditions, standards and values of each people cannot be disregarded.[6] The Asian states in the Bangladesh Declaration of April 1993, underlined: "while human rights are universal in nature, they must be considered in the context of a dynamic and evolving process of international norm-setting, bearing in mind the significance of national and regional particularities and various historical, cultural and religious backgrounds".[7]

Very contrary to other countries, Chinese delegation, even, questioned the universality of human rights. This was balanced however by the assurance that the Chinese government complies with the principles formulated in the UN Charter and Universal Declaration of Human Rights.

Thus the Vienna Declaration adopted by consensus of the World Conference confirmed the universality of human rights and rejected the notion of cultural relativism. The Declaration, in its paragraph 1, reaffirms the solemn commitment of all states to fulfil their obligations to promote universal respect for and observance and protection of all human rights and fundamental freedoms for all. It stress: "The universal nature of these rights, and freedoms is beyond question".

The problems of national and regional peculiarities is referred to in paragraph 5 of the Declaration which provides:

> "All human rights are universal, indivisible and inter-dependent and inter-related . . . while the significance of national and regional peculiarities and various historical, cultural and religious backgrounds must be borne in mind, it is the duty of states, regardless of their political, economic and cultural systems, to promote and protect all human rights and fundamental freedoms."

The results of the Vienna Conference confirm that cultural relativism is in retreat on many fronts[8]. This is important not only for the debate concerning the universality of human rights but also in a more general context for international relations. Rejecting cultural relativism and recognizing at the same time the significance of cultural specificities, the Vienna Conference intensified the discussion concerning relation between cultural values and human rights. This has been articulated, in particular, in the debate concerning the so-called 'Asian Values'. Begun by the Bangkok Declaration of 1993, animated by declarations and statements of the governments of China, Malaysia, Indonesia and Singapore, the debate quickly surpassed the governmental level and is now conducted at various seminars and in specialised literatures.[9]

By keeping above details in our mind, we come to understand that majority countries of the world, most probably third and fourth world people realised that homogenisation in the form of language, cloths, style of dressing and advertising is utilised by globalisation as an industry with large profit. So the challenges or contradiction 'between cultural determinism and cultural relativism could be seen in the global scenario. So eminent Marxist scholar Aijaj Ahmad rightly remarked "Globalisation unites the market and divides human beings, because human beings can be best used for purposes of the global marketing if they act as individual consumers and not as a people in solidarity with each other. Post-modernism on a global scale, and post-colonial theory in relation to the third world, are the main instruments in this battle to replace the polity of equality with the politics of differences, the society of cooperation by the society of infinite competition, class consciousness vs. community consciousness." Even it hurts to the concept of nationalism as consequence, the scale of ethnic-nationalism and ethno-culturalism are articulated as separatist movement on large scale within the nation.

In case of regional development in India; it has three major aims (productive, social and biological). It was an attempt to secure best condition and possibilities for an all-round development for everybody: minimize and ultimately eliminate inter-regional and intra-regional differences in quality of life and make the best possible use of natural resources, land, human values of the region to secure the production and social aims. These aims are comprehensive in nature and not restricted to economic (productive) aspects alone. They emphasize on distributive justice so that the differences in levels of living could be eliminated creating conditions for all-round development of all people of the regions. The philosophical foundation of such policy should therefore be based on cooperation rather than on competition whereas the multinationals' mandate for globalisation, liberalisation and structural adjustment is the philosophical outcome of the "survival of the fittest".

It should be remembered that the social structure of the developing societies whether conceived in the national or regional levels is inhibitive of progress. The benefits of increased development in economic and social activities in these areas go to those who need them least. But investments to raise the level of living of the people should percolate downwards, upwards, sideways so that everybody gets benefit. This leads to better participation of all people in productive activities. Nobody progresses unless all progress and co-operations and mutual support should orient the development policies. Surplus productions would naturally get recycled for mutual benefit or in an inter-regional system gets invested in other regions to bring about inter-regional equity in development.

The description of our kind of development should therefore be the processes through which a society acquires greater porosity within its own body politic and enables its members to gain greater control over themselves and their environment. For this, the primary considerations should be transforming the social structures and institutions especially restructuring production, changes in social structure, cultural change and changes in political and legal structure. Then only an economy can be geared to ensure productive employment for the whole population. The provision of health, education and similar other facilities is only a secondary aspect of social development which may be necessary but neither sufficient nor possible except making any headway in transforming social structure making our permeable society to a porous one.

The aims of regional development mentioned above need a comprehensive social development policy suitable for a developing country like India. But regional development encompassing not only productivity and income but also structural change in class and interest group relations, so that broad masses of working people are able to participate and sharing in productivity leading to increase welfare, in gross as well as 'net' terms should be the prescription of development. For this, policy of increasing growth automatically trickling down below canvassed till now, should be rejected.

The inadequacy of prevalent theories and practices of regional development (mostly disaggregated version of western macro-economic growth models) is that, development is conceived nearly in terms of study growth of production and income whereas social class interest and group relations which form the basis of distribution of the gains of development are assumed to change with increase in productivity. Human beings are treated not as goal but as factors of production and recipients of particular marginal investment through public expenditure in social welfare programmes such as health, education, housing, social security and so on. Social policies therefore reduced to operational allocation of various residual resources derived from national system for redistribution and for partially covering the accumulated deficit in certain welfare services. The government as well as academia by and large accepts globalisation as inevitable in plea of TINA (There is no alternative). If that is so, one is to accept that policies for national or regional development are irrelevant in the wake of globalisation. In case of International policy options the question of relevance of state is also dubious. At one level the state is being resisted by ethnic and other groups pressing for greater autonomy and self-determination. At other level, they are being bypassed by MNCs who give a damn to local jurisdiction. So AK Maity (Globalisation *vis-a-vis* Regional Development, p.49) stated that "States therefore become too big for the small things and too small for the big". In short, international bodies like International Monetary Fund, World Bank and World Trade Organisation could wipe away national borders and wipe out national policies for development, be it national or in regional plans.

Globalisation and Cultural Commodification

The response of individual countries to globalisation is different, but ethnic revival was on the rise in the nineties everywhere. In many countries globalisation underlined question of the unjust redistribution of goods and greater impoverishment. The issue of social justice led to the idea of "equality" of the collectivity of a homogenous nation. The new social democracy controls the government with the help of a selected elite, which supports neoliberalism and globalisation, like the right. Their bureaucratic and technocratic mode of communication isolates them from the population. The state under left or right withdraws into a role of guarding security and this transforms social life, turning democracy into a hostage. It leads emergence of ethno-nationalism in India particularly in NE in spite of having maximum efforts in the process of nation building.

Emergence of caste war in India in general and ethnic war particularly in NE are also impact of globalisation. In the process of globalisation every domains of country could be deemed by super-imposition of highly developed countries. Basically, culture is a composite behaviour pattern of the human being which is given by many factors. Dynamics of cultural change is given by education, information, administration, besides the economic factors of income and social security. Culture undergoes change over time when these perspective change. When Manipuris were converted to *Vaishnavism* there was physical appearance and presence of Shantidas Gosai. But to-day without such physical appearance, people are socialised by world channel in *their* drawing rooms. Western education (not 'regional oriented), illusive socialisation through global channel with new mode of life and administration brought about vast changes in the age-old culture of the various traditional societies of NE state. Nevertheless, if all evils of cultural types including folk society, feudal society and patrilineal could be changed through modern scientific and technological innovation, to some extent that is good. But these are still in the mindsets of all. It is said that new cars swept the small roads; mobiles in our pockets and world channels in our drawing rooms but still mindsets are in parochial. That is why, orthodox assertions could be denoted on large scale and reactions are also there. But on the other hand the people of the region are in the trap of cultural commodification of the globalisation. People are not concerned with the question of unemployment instead they are facing of job losing. Their indigenous products are completely at the outside of the markets. That means they are also economically marginalised day by day. Now, the question is how the institution of labour relations receptive to competitive development, as is prescribed by contemporary economic reforms given by the globalisation and how many states in India including NE states, the agrarian relations are receptive to agrarian reforms? But we are all putting on western dress, imitating western food and using all types of cosmetics.

During the Seven-Year Devastation (1819-26), when Manipur was occupied by *Ava*, swords in the hands of the men-folk who were protecting their motherland, were replaced by *Cortana* for *Sankritana* of Vaishnavism. Moreover, in the careless moment, our *penakhongbas* simply mentioned the fnaple of *Kunjamala* in the epic of *Khamba-Thoibi*. But to-day Khamba-Thoibi seems to be written after Hindu Conversion i.e. after 17th century. That means, cultural assimilation either forcibly or in soft-line, the ultimate losers are the underdeveloped countries and indigenous people.

So the question is that the inter-cultural dynamics in the contemporary process of globalisation consolidated various cultural and ethical values in order to bring common culturalism. But the interpretation of common culturalism is completely based on economic basis. The tacit tussle is going on. The hidden agenda of cultural relativism and cultural commodification is on top priority. Thus, the economic festeration of the periphery is in the process of non-stop to dig up their graves. It is the reality of globalisation for all third and fourth world countries. That is why the periphery demos are in demegration with challenging tendencies.

Lastly, no one could ignore the negative impact of cultural relativism and cultural commodification in the process of the new world order like globalisation because the problem faced by the people of this region such as ethno-nationalism, ethnic conflicts, demographic transformations are impact of these global orders. Therefore, we the people of Northeast in general and Manipur in particular, far lagging behind in all fronts, should reject universalised cultural relativism, we should also challenge against the cultural commodification which was super imposed by the advanced countries of the world, ruling elites and local collaborators of the imperialist globalisation. Unless there is check and balance the dream of another world is impossible.

NOTES

1. Ashok Kumar Maiti, S: "Globalisation vis-a-vis Regional Development, Challenges before the North Eastern States" in *Development Priorities in North East India*, Edited by Bimal J. Deb. Concept, Delhi, 2002, p 4l.
2. Brzezinki, "The New Challenges to Human Rights", *Journal of Democracy*, 8(2) April 1995, p4.
3. Janusz Symoniodes, *New Human Rights Dimension, Obstacles and Challenges*, New Delhi, 2003, p.24.
4. Our Creative Diversity, Report of the World Commission on Cultural and Development, UNESCO, 1995, p. 55.

5. DOC.AlCONF.157/AFRM/14.
6. *DOC.AlCONF*. 157/ASRM/7.
7. *DOC.AlCONF*. 157/ASRM/7.
8. A. Etzioni, "The End of Cross-Cultural Relativism" *Alternatives*, 22, 1997, p.l77.
9. J. Bauer, "International Human Rights and Asian Commitment", *Human Rights Dialogue*, December 1995.
10. *Social Science* 32(9-10): 376-377, Sept.-Oct., 2004.

3

Globalisation and Cultural Encounters: The Manipuri Perspective

—LOKENDRA ARAMBAM

Introduction

Globalisation is now the most 'happening' event in the light of vast changes taking place throughout the world, when the economies of nation-states open out to mutual integration processes through principles of deregulation, privatization and liberalization, thereby effecting structural adjustments in tune with the logic of global capitalism. In the words of one Indian Industrialist Rahul Bajaj, 'More liberalization and de-regulation of the Indian economy is needed. Globalisation is inevitable. There is no alternative'. This mindset reflected the change in the economic policies of the Indian state, which started with the liberalization programme by Prime Minister Narasimha Rao in 1991. Now the present government of Prime Minister Manmohan Singh proclaimed the concretization of the Look East Policy, initiated by the former Prime Minister in 1996. This shall mean, as a follow up from the Kunming initiative of 1989 (where late Prime Minister Rajiv Gandhi played a very important role) a greater regional cooperation in economic and cultural matters such as between Bangladesh, India, Myanmar and China (BIMC). India is looking towards the transformation of Northeast India for a greater economic and cultural integration with the Southeast Asian countries, while remaining politically as an integral part of India (Ramesh, 2004). What shall be the likely ramifications of this new trend of thought and action on the Manipuri people as a whole may form the key issue of this address. The exercise has however its own limitations, since the material history of the subject of study is yet inadequate for a proper objective discourse to develop, and we have to depend on speculative sociological insights to form a proper viewpoint on the same. Also Globalisation per se had been debated upon extensively in contemporary social science discourses, but Manipur has yet to grasp fully its implications and ramifications in a conflict ridden environment. Economists of the state speak about it often, but we have yet to articulate the very processes of Globalisation (another term may be modernization under contemporary capitalist transformation) and its impact upon traditional ethnic societies (of which we are part), and on people and polities who had experienced the historical burden of imperialism and colonialism. Any studies of social science or the humanities and their cross-disciplinary interactions have to undergo an intense examination of how we as people responded to imperialism and colonialism. Developments since then in subsequent historical periods also reflect veneers of that colonial impact on our values, ideals and forms of knowledge, and successive political and cultural patterns we manifested was reflective of our having undergone experiences of bondage, subjugation and subordination. Our relationship with the Indian state since 1949, and the succession to the power vacuum created by the dissembling British Empire by the modern Indian state, and the logic of its national development as a third world power incorporated hegemonistic interventions in the so-called peripheries, resulting in re-creation of earlier imperial and colonial processes, thereby resulting in the advent of serious challenges to its legitimacy and political authority. The problems of contemporary Manipuri peoples agonies are therefore the crisis created by unequal development untrue to its status and dignity, undermined by an inadequate national discourse of post-colonial India, whose incorporation of the ancient Asiatic state destroyed its originary structures and energies. Manipur's development in the wake of the fresh onslaughts of globalisation and its interventionist role under a coercive Indian state shall be of greater incoherence and disequilibrium noticed in violence all-around the social and moral world of the ethnic societies. Globalisation discourse had not depicted any all-round development of ordinary people. In the words of Koves, 'The new historical phase of imperialism, globalisation destroys the fabric of human societies; claims to go back to roots and essences which support fascisization in various forms' (Koves, 2004). Also as the pressures of the global era on the state increase, there were less possibilities for implementation of social policies, and making of decisions that result in a more equal distribution of income (Sijuwade, 2004). What India showed as a result of liberalization and globalisation, was how it 'had been subjected to economic reforms to an increased duality of growth experiences during the 1990's-high growth rates of the secondary and tertiary sectors in a few states enjoying large advantages in terms of industrial locations and infrastructures, and low growth rates in the poor states with a high burden of poverty and stagnation'. (*Ibid.*, 2004).

Retrogression in Culture

The economic impact of globalisation has been studied by many contemporary social scientists, and the results show symptomatic patterns of the power hungry middle class aggressively slave-driving the productive forces of society, disinvesting unwanted labour, creating social anomie and compromising on welfare measures and leaving nothing for the poor and the weak. Productivity is the key word, and massive unemployment, closure of avenues of livelihood, and sheer attrition in living and meeting the challenges of consumer expenditure from inadequate incomes, thereby impacting on young and ignorant lives to become violent and demanding are the social phenomena for peripheral economies of states like the Northeast. In spite of some local productivity in agriculture in the sixties and seventies, Manipur had witnessed a recession and stress since the nineties, which is symptomatic of the pinching impact of India's economic programmes, which had resulted to the increase in violence in society. The blame for the anarchic condition and social disequilibrium are heaped upon 'insurgency', without however taking into account the massive corrosion of values, ideals and moral of the governing class, the corruption in the government and institutions, and destruction of collective life through inorganic developmentalism enforced from the logic of the centre for rearranging the periphery at its behest. New social and economic classes had risen to political and social power, but this new class, which did not have any relationship with core traditional values and ethics had become rapid operators of mercenary onslaughts through economic opportunism and corruption. These classes are at the helm of public affairs. The younger generation of students, youths who are in forefront of public movements are also devoid of any civilizational linkage with tradition, and adolescents in society are bereft of familial and social ties, due to the retreat of parental care, concern and interaction. The system of modern education are heavily structured for enhanced dependence for enslavement of minds, rather than for freeing the intellect from routine knowledge and perpetuation of received ideas. The new individual, which had been severed from its moorings in the collectivity of the Asian past, is under-developed and ill defined. Yet he is presumed to be the pillar of the contemporary democratic polity, when he is however motivated by sinister self-interest, self-aggrandizing habits, and is prone to intrigue and back-stabbing culture, which are traits brought in by India's educational and cultural influences. The character of the Manipuri individual had been transformed rapidly since the incorporation of the state into the Indian Union, and the subsequent historical experience in the era of 'development'. Primordial passions of conflictual duality (Anee Thokpee), incompatibility and personal equations of jealousy and rancour amongst leading social, political and intellectual elites, non-communication amongst colleagues in spite of space sharing in institutions and pro-modern establishments reflect the transformed character of the Manipuri individual. Small egos had been boosted like that of the frog in the well, due to false operation of influence and patronage from the central institutions of power.

This cultural transformation in a retrogade manner, in inverse proportion to modernization processes had not been critically reviewed in any of our public discourses. Modernization theorists presume modern values to include 'an openness to new experience, readiness for social change, orientation towards the future, efficacy, long-term planning, valuing technical skills, and educational and occupational aspirations (Inkeles and Smith, 1974). All these are not simply happening. On the other hand, it is right to agree with Dependency theorists that economic and cultural dependence only produces the 'development of underdevelopment' (Frank, 1969, Galtung, 1975). Manipur now reflects an intense example of forcible underdevelopment in modern times, a fall from a high degree of indigenous civilizational experience in pre-colonial times reflected in its 'national' ethos built up in some two thousand years of sheer tryst with history. Why this is so is the profound question of the day.

The probable answer by leading official policy planners on the issues of the decay or decline of societal and civilizational mores are laid on the doors of massive 'political violence' created by conflict and insurgency. Violence, or propensity to damage the body of the other is not only the pre-occupation of the non-state actors, but also of the ruthless suppressive presence of the coercive Indian state, whose combined impact on society had revealed the tragedy of contemporary Manipuri society. Violence is not simply a physical act destroying the body or life of the individual in society, but it accompanies the structural disintegration of norms, institutions and social universes, which are not properly visible due to the resilience of tradition. The insides of the polity are gradually corroding, due to the complex networks of the corrupt civil, military, police and bureaucracy whose combined onslaughts into the realm of power and resources are destroying all semblance of democratic aspirations. Both state and non-state actors are mutually unleashing a stranglehold on the fragile lived-experiences of the people. A cold and benumbing presence is reflected in the moral and social world, and an atmosphere of silence (Le de Silencio) pervades in the public sphere (in spite of severe ferocity of agitations and demonstrations). Sheer violence of confrontation, attrition and mutual acrimony destroys the equilibrium of extended households, constituencies and human settlements of artificially created boundaries, through the demands of heavily monetized electoral politics, and veteran politicians often experience mental and physical wreckage and trauma. Women activists who struggle to protect the innocent son from the onslaught of the instruments of the Indian state often die unnoticed deaths from complex traumatic experience unleashed in the Meira-Paibee movement. Sheer epistemic violence is noticed in the interstices of family, language, culture and behavioural norms and the entire originary world of the autochthons are ruptured beyond repair. The Manipuris do not live their lives, they live the life of others. Such is the character of the transformation of the Manipuri in the world of global capitalism.

Politics of Culture and Identity

What consumes the contemporary civilization of the people of Manipur is the advent of cultural re-configuration of politics through the principle of ethnicity or the politics of identity, severely accentuated by the global scenario of reckless motivation for access to power, resources and territory by groups and communities. Ethnic identity, which propelled the individual to affiliate to the group, which became a global concern after the end of the cold war were impelled by the struggle by elite formations in their search for space and dignity in the global rush for re-distribution of spoils after the aftermath of imperialism. Imperialism however had not ended with the shrinkage of the erstwhile European states with their vast networks of rule over alien populations and territories. The system of rule and the cultural and behavioural forms of knowledge created by empires left vestiges of their influence on the natives who sought re-empowerment of their re-discovered selves in the new environment of economic competition and survival of the fittest. Ethnic categories which existed in plural orders were enabled to assert themselves for power and resources through strong mobilizational networks on the principle of primordial consciousness. Though British imperialism created ethnic difference amongst the multiple plurality of the Manipur societies in pre-colonial times, it was the successor Indian state which ensophisticated the ethnic divide amongst the Manipuris by differential treatment amongst the ethnic groups, balancing out and playing upon the weaknesses and prejudices of the aroused ethnic communities. The policies of the Indian state over the peoples of the Northeast under the principle of National security in the wake of insurgency are replete with intrigues, manoeuvres, and advantage seeking for self-perpetuation through severe and sinister manipulation of ethnic jealousy amongst the communities in the Northeast. Cultural identity which could have been positive values for human development had been re-arranged and re-structured for mutual hostilities and rancour, that the successor state would use it to self-perpetuate their hold over peoples of the Northeast. All ethnic unrest in the Northeast are not simple by-products of European Imperialism, but are enhanced by policies of Hinterland Imperialism propagated silently by the Indian state under the official hegemonic discourse of 'Development'.

Under such conditions of suppression, directed developmentalism and coercive rule under the official discourse of National Integration and development, what exactly shall be the profile of the cultural encounter faced by the people of Manipur in the fresh wake of globalisation and the Look East Policy of the Indian state? The answers shall not lie in the narratives of the obvious impact of circulation of global cultures, of rap music, dress styles of the young, or the homogenized images and practices of consumerism, now making a stranglehold on the economy of arrested production in Manipur. The answers must be sought on the state of 'intellectual haemorrhage' already suffered by the Manipuri people, where the second colonial experience of Indian rule had drained the minds of the Manipuris of all contents of reality. One has only to study the colonial experience of the African tribal societies which had been extensively debated upon by African intellectuals like Fannon, Aime-Caesare, Nguigi-wa-Thiongo, Wole Soyinka and others which had not reached the intellectual domain of the university teachers and faculties in this forlorn state. The representation of the Manipuri intellectual shall need intense analysis and introspection, since they had not lived up to the challenges thrown open by massive onslaughts of dehumanization spawned on the people as a whole by the discourse of development.

For now the Manipuris need a higher form of experience and knowledge to unearth the true genius of the Manipuri people which had been subsumed under the contemporary culture of the second Indianization. The first phase of Indianization resorted to severe state violence accompanied by attempt to destroy native learning and philosophy by the burning of the puyas, physical torture of conscientious objectors, desecration of places of indigenous worship, destruction of native idols and tremendous arousal of primal passions, contests and debates on values and principles. Yet the national war being fought against the expanding Burman Empire in the eighteenth century brought the lineages, clans and tribes together under the banner of the ethno-national formation, and the Manipur experience was of high civilizational energy. The sensuous, diplomatic efforts of Bhagyachandra did not result in what contemporary scholars term the Hinduization of the Meitei, but rather the Meeteization of Hinduism, which is intrinsically different in meaning and emphasis from the earlier concept. The assimilation and synthesizing experiences did not accompany a hegemonic relationship with the core culture's domain in the Indian heartland, which enabled the ruling classes of Manipur to devise ways and means of indigenous response to world cultures and influences. What was drastically different was the defeat of the national state in 1891, which created a system of dependence to the colonial power in the centre, thereby beginning the patterns of relationship between core and periphery, ruler and subject with varying degrees of response, in the anti-colonial awakenings of the early twentieth century. The British Empire decimated the military strength of the lineage aristocracy, started social-engineering processes for creation of a subservient colonial order, and encouraged cultural production which was not subversive of the new hegemony. However Imperialism could not destroy the strength and resilience of Manipuri women, who withstood the forces of exploitation and dominance by resorting to direct political activism and resistance in the two women's wars of the early twentieth century. The ethnic brethren also resisted the penetration of colonial rule and exploitation resulting in the Anglo-Kuki War of 1917-19, and Jadonang Gaidinlieu movement in 1932-34. All these struggles were suppressed through military interventions by the central power authority of the Empire.

The second wave of Indianization starting from the early secularization and democratization processes of the Mahasabha era was a transformation from hegemony through consent to ruthless subversion of indigenous development, thereby resulting in suppression of native dignity, pride and history, systematic degradation of the political status of the post-imperial state was organized through modern Indian subtlety, intrigue and intimidation. After the integration of the Manipur state into the Indian Union in 1949, the first step taken towards incorporation of the people to the mainstream was the cancellation of the Foreigners Registration Act, which had earlier attempted to regulate entry of other demographic components and racial categories, so as to preserve the identity and protect the weak work ethic of the native populations. The new sense of Indianism propagated by the Indian rulers was to make the virgin states of the Northeast share the national burden of partition which affected the future social and economic scenario of simple polities of Tripura, Assam, Manipur and the Northeast. Large scale influx of refugees, internally and externally displaced populations from the eastern Indian semi-heartland was to shift the demographic, economic and political environment of the Northeast towards conflictual alignment and attrition. Earlier, the states of the Northeast were extremely humanitarian in their outlook and character, and rulers like Bodhchandra of Manipur and Vikram Chandra Manikya of Tripura were exemplary in their attitudes towards the refugees of war and partition, and there were little animosity towards the ethnic order. Sheer ethnic hatred, and competition over resources and territory were the gift of the Indian state, with their insidious presence and influence through political, business and military actions. The character of counter-insurgency operations in Nagaland, Manipur, Mizoram and Tripura shall reveal the racist paradigms of distance, mistrust and suspicion, which blocked out awareness of the development of an 'other' people in history. Large scale napalm bombing in Nagaland, rape of its women, decapacitation of not only the 'hostile' insurgents but widespread destruction of homes, family and property accompanied the counter-insurgency operations. The Indian Air Force was extensively utilized to counter the Mizo insurgents, and forcible grouping of villages, displacement of ethnic populations, and twentieth century violations of rights to life and security were perpetuated before the international rights activism was in the ascendant, and thus the question of engagement with the North easterner people were not based on principles of natural justice. The Indian state had another brutal mind, in spite of proclamations of the 21st century Pan-Indian national ethos propelled by the aspirations to become a global player in Asia. This double face, this double-speak (what one politician says one and does the other in different spaces) has been an innate trait of the new Indian political and business classes who are in league with ethnic elites of the North Eastern states. The character of the Indian democratic classes in league with political elites are representative of the new Indianism, when the resources and properties of the virgin states are open to appropriation and exploitation for mutual benefit, and the linkages of the mainstream leaders with the willing compradors of the native states have sinister implications for the health of the polities. Even some national parties were funded from the illicit economy of drug and contraband goods accruing from the highly internationalized (globalized) transactions of global capital with transit through the interiors of Manipur and the North East.

The failure of the state to eke out any welfare measures for the people, the insidious cutting off of funds by the centre for even routine expenditures of the government, and ethnicization of poverty which is taking place are normally blamed on the disequilibrium created by insurgency. Yet at the same time, emergence of lumpen elements in the social sphere, the link between adventurers and self seekers with the high authorities of state, corruption in police, bureaucracy and the institutions are not caused by the insurgents alone. They are all products of a system spawned by what is proclaimed as 'Development', but which has unread and unspoken about dynamics in the operation of socio-economic processes. What the development jargon had undertaken was to corrupt the leading economic, social and political classes, continue the framework of democracy, under which all forms of oppression, exclusivism, ethnic prejudices, could be aroused, pacified, played upon, and manipulated without the knowledge of the humanized world.

Look East for What?

What then could be the new challenge of opening out culturally and economically to the affluent states of East and Southeast Asia, though with some contradictory attachment to an intriguing polity of Myanmar? Globalisation, though is a new term, connected mainly with economic paradigms of capital shift and focus, free flow of goods, services and knowledge, but cultural and societal patterns, relationships and engagements had been taking place in one form or another throughout the historical experiences of Manipuri people. Having had originary historical experiences from the cultural East, the Manipuris should be proud of re-locating itself in the promised opening of the Eastern Door (Nongpok Thong Haangba). Wisdom teachers like Chingoo Khongnangthaba had come and gone, but their apocalyptic visions through sheer meditative practices and spiritual discipline had seen the evils of opening up of the Western door. The new imagined connection with the East has some practical implications which shall wash away false pride and soarings of ethnic imagination however.

For what the Look East Policy of the Indian state entails is there shall be material transformation in the infrastructures of roads, railways, hydro-electric resources, and trade between the adjacent countries like China, Thailand and other South East Asian states shall be enhanced within agreed patterns of socio-economic principles seminally formed in the Kunming enclave of 1989. It shall involve, first the finishing off of insurgent elements physically (through UN Human Rights bodies advised political approaches), permanent stationing of the two thousand odd kilometre long sub-Himalayan ranges in the international border by the Indian military, the luring of transnational corporations whose sole motivation was of profit and profit only after proper road, rail and air connectivity between the states of the promised regional zone of economic cooperation had been materialized. Cultural productions emanating from the native in the forms of dances, music, theatre and the arts shall have an unrestricted flow and exchange which may benefit the cultural workers of the state. More trading shall follow, with mutual competition between the regional manufacturing and industrial centres, which shall heighten the quality of the goods in competition.

However, what shall be the role of ethnic populations who are, and still shall remain, in the global periphery, with an unequal exchange system in the praxis of livelihood and material existence? What role of participation, or decision making in polity concerns had ever been empowered to the natives? Who are the institutional heads of governments, and how many sons of soil are recruited in the decision making bodies in governance, in development departments, and in civil and military establishments? What really constitutes the natural, indigenous development of the region, without exogenous control and direction? What represents Manipuri reality? Is Manipuri reality conceived, inscribed and perceived by the contemporary Indian state, or is it another form of reality which exists in the nerves and veins of the Manipuri people? Who benefits from the new Indianism, a sense of belonging to India's new nationhood, leaving aside or forgetting the atrocities perpetrated by the security agencies against innocent men and women who bear the agonies of the violence between the state and non-state actors? Are the Non-state actors aware of the deeper implications of the Look East Policy and obvious semiotic influences of the recent counter-insurgency operations? The tumultous disarray and disequilibrium which is likely to occur when the state is in internal war with political dissidents, and the sociological syndrome of 'dysarchy' when the forces against the powerful state often fall into factionalism and divisiveness because of the sheer power of the state are in operation, shall have to re-structure their thoughts and ideas of human emancipation in the grand design of coercive hegemony under the discourse of development. The Northeastern states, including Manipur, are rapidly transforming into fascist comprador states with greater infiltration into the private lives of democratic citizens, and the emergence of a great South Asian power as a Police state is in the offing. Civil liberties are under threat again. Portents of globalisation!

These are some of the issues implied by the recent overture to global capitalism. The obvious fears of Chinese economic expansionism, and their conversion of Myanmar into a Chinese satellite state had provoked the foregrounding of the Look East Policy. One must remember the reality of Chinese neo-colonial practices on Myanmar, that the northern Shan states like Lashio, Myitkina, Bhamo etc. had already been colonized by Chinese moneyed immigrants, and ethnic Shan and other populations had withdrawn into the suburbs and villages. The Salween river systems had been modernized to carry heavy mercantile shipping, and China is also planning modernization of the Irawaddy and Chindwin river systems too.

In the words of Robb (2003) a contemporary Myanmar watcher, 'Burmese people in regions close to the Chinese border, are understandably less comfortable with the increasing foreign presence in their traditional territories. At the most immediate level, recent reports describe rising real estate prices in northeastern cities, to the point where long term residents are being forced into satellite towns and villages, when main cities begin to look like Chinese colony-towns' (*China Rights Forum Journal*, May 2003).

Looking at the way modern states exercising sovereignty in international relations, do exploit peripheral regions as captive populations, and how the latter experience deep processes of national hurt and wounded historical dignity, we may reflect that the Manipuris may continue to remain as simple carriers of goods and services without developing qualitative entrepreneurial enterprize to benefit from the proposed economic cooperation between the regions. The atmosphere at the recently developed Moreh town, which had become a melting pot of social inequilibrium because of absence of a long rootedness in community life may become indicators of the new scenario in the era of globalisation. So also is Dimapur as a complex of commercial activities, where community culture had not built up traditional forms of inter-dependence and sanity, and the new townships spawned by the money economy shall witness deeply delicate imbalances in social and cultural relationships, always prone to violence and conflict. It is however not to deny that some pragmatic solutions are worked by the inter-ethnic stakeholders in the economy, but that is not enough for rapidly transforming economic centres in the harsh, competitive world unleashed by global capitalism.

Witnessing grassroot experiences of people, economy and culture along the national highway reflect various forms of adaptation and change in traditional communities when economic imperatives impel new formation of townships, relegation to oblivion of traditional places of ritual or cultural importance, and subsequent human interactions taking place in newly constituted districts and centres of administration and governance. The newly constituted districts of Senapati hide ugly features of ethnic distance, alienation of major hill populations from other ethnic brethren, an almost complete closure to plains interaction at the administrative infra-structures and subsequent governance initiatives. Incidents of closure of government offices and institutions, cultural affiliation to the neighbouring state and repeated economic blockades of the highway traffic, pressure to faceless transport operators are some of the regular symptoms of ethnic divide, of policies of identity and difference, which are being played upon by non-state forces and the security agencies. The peoples alienation from the plains brothers had reached unenviable stages of possible conflict, which civil societies at both levels had not succeeded to mitigate. Ethnic variables amongst other indigenes also hinge upon resorting to arms to safeguard clan, lineage or group interests. Other expatriate communities like the Nepalis also sustain delicate balance in the mutually suspicious environment, and the propensity to resort to arms are not the exception amidst marginal communities. Groups and other ethnic minorities often subvert their traditional identities or historical origins in order to affiliate with bigger tribes who could promise more material and moral aid, protect their interests in the insidious political manouvres. The impact of the economy, the necessity for survival and safeguarding of group interests often impact upon issues of identity, and the ethnic balance are poised at a critical level of rupture and fission created by the modern economy. Small ethnic communities shall no longer remain voiceless, passive witnesses to the changing socio-economic scenario. Ethnic identity shall remain the unavoidable plank for tribal mobilization and assertion for power and resources.

Cultural Conflict and Suppressing Mutualities

The emergence of the national construction of Naga identity and the recent the political negotiation with the GOI on the one side, and the furious confrontation of the Indian security agencies with the militant non-state actors in the southeast and southwestern regions of Manipur bordering Myanmar are two vital subjects upon which Manipuri intellectuals and the academic circles are unable to express a view point, which is the unfortunate reminder to the marginalization of the literati in popular discourse of the day. The sensitivity of the subject, the environment of insecurity, and the hold of the non-state and state forces and their coercive hold on territory and population, and the presence of the elements of fear psychosis and the disastrous destruction of democratic principles and practice by the instruments of the Indian state in their violations over life and security, the hidden alignment of non-state groups within the subterranean regions of politics and insurgency are some of the vital factors which inhibit frank discussion on the subjects. The issues of Naga's claim to nationhood cannot be wished away as a figment of imagination of a long oppressed community, but the context of their 'destabilization' of former territorial concepts and frames of geography and culture are uneasy claims which the major community from the plains could not easily let by. In the massive agitation on the cease-fire issue in June 2001, some eighteen lives were lost, yet the plains community did not possess an adversarial attitude towards the Naga brethren, which reflected ingredients of plural community which the pre-colonial state cherished, but which had been dented by hierarchical attitudes developed by world religions, and through unenlightened ethnic prejudiced policies pursued by the comprador classes spawned by the Indian electoral system of democratic rule. The grievances on both sides are not democratically discussed amongst the ethnic communities themselves, but were left to the indifferent, self-perpetuating arbiters of New Delhi, who had no other principles other than play upon native weaknesses. The major plains viewpoint realistically stem from the simple logic of some 20% of the population claiming 75% of the territory and geography of the state, which is also inhabited by other ethnic components, and the fact of how 66 per cent of the population concentrated on one-tenth of the geographical area, which itself has extensive demographic pressures on land would consider reconstitution of ethnic states when multi-ethnicity and pluralism should become a fact of post-colonial life, is the major historical reality of the moment. Ethnicity and Ethnic identity and politics of culture would have been major historical subjects on state formation, which problem the issues of globalisation shall accentuate.

The other issue of militarization of parts of the Manipur state are propelled by the necessity for pragmatic implementation of the Look East Policy of the Indian state in the context of globalisation and integration of the economies of sub-regional groupings like BIMC, which enabled the Indian state, flushed from the Bhutan Operation of 2003, to undertake this exclusive counter-insurgency operation under the pretext of Prime Minister Manmohan Singh's diplomatic tour of the Northeast in Nov. 2004. The issues become important since the Indian state has been severely jolted by the 9/11 syndrome, the attack on Parliament, and the communal divide between communities, and more importantly, the strong emergence of left-extremism in the heartland. The recent developments in the heartland, when the Maoist Communist Party from Nepal, the Maoist Communist Centre from Bihar, and the Peoples War Group from Andhra Pradesh and Tamil Nadu are reported to have forged an alliance termed 'Compact Revolutionary Zone', which had corrected the earlier Naxalite mistakes of the late Charu Majumdar from the 1969-71 experience. The fast emergence of left extremism due to the hegemonic concentration of power and resources by some three hundred million middle class, the communal divide between Hindus and Muslims as a result of politicization of religion, the internationalization of the dispute over Kashmir, and the mushrooming ethnic insurgencies in the Northeast were the compelling features of the hard look at the National security issue. Though the economy of the Indian state was fast developing to counter China's hegemony over Asia, the logic of the capitalist transformation compelled the Indian state to assume the character of a Police state where coercive and suppressive measures against internal subversion were to be the exercised, the defence forces had secured a vital space in the decision making power structure, since the 9/11 tragedy and global terrorism became the political counterpart of the economic term. While economic integration benefits the fast developing social class, the global network of 'Terrorism' whose meaning had been subsumed without the principle of distinction being applied, should be finished off. Physical elimination was the key, which prompted conscientious journalists of Tehelka to reveal corruption in the defence forces, and also the issue of how body counts became the watchword for upward mobility and career achievements for the rank and file in the armed forces. Such is the atmosphere under which the Armed Forces Special Powers Act 1958, a colonial and imperial legacy, was utilized in the Northeast. Repressive contemporary political culture then is the hallmark of the suppressor regimes which was ushered by economic development. The compulsions of Look East Policy necessitated the new counter-insurgency operations, where the insurgents of Manipur should have to be wiped off, or forced to resort to 'negotiation' through conflict fatigue, and then subsume them through prolonged attrition within the temptations the Asian global power could provide. The character of the Indian state as a modern Leviathan should have to be studied by social science researchers engaged in the project of politics and culture in the era of global capitalism.

This issue then raises the fundamental question of how political morality and international humanitarian laws should operate to protect basic dignity, security and the inalienable rights of the human being embroiled in conflict. Customary International humanitarian law provides essential 'principles of proportionality' whereby the measures undertaken by State

Parties to counter threats to national security should not be beyond the level or intensity produced by the non-state actors. In a sense, what the force or equipments used by the state should be in proportion to that used by the non-state actors. Also the principle of distinction should be exercised to discriminate who are the combatants and non-combatants. Also the principle of time limitation in a sense of how states of emergency should not be continued too long, that excessive extension of repressive laws tend to become permanent thereby infringing upon basic inalienable rights of the human being to live with dignity and security. In the era of globalisation, when economic integration had become the universal principle, the matter of how international morality and respect for human rights are being denied is a serious moral and ethical question, that cultural values in democracy and justice should emphasize. The manner how the Indian state does not ratify the additional protocols of the ICCPR and ICESCR, as well as the Additional Protocols of the Geneva Conventions reflect on the attitude of the Indian government on issues of National Security *vis-a-vis* Human rights and International Humanitarian Law, which any State Party joining the bandwagon of Globalisation should, as a moral principle, practice in order to respect basic democratic values. The state's function as a re-distributive institution of justice had been undermined in dealing with questions of conflict and violence. Also, in this global era of intense violence, civil wars, and internal wars, the global concern for respect for human dignity cannot be brushed aside from the simple reason of internal security, and international debates on how state sovereignty should be curbed to establish the rights of society and the human individual had been in full swing. Any one interested on this issue appreciate the contribution of Michael Foucault in developing this international discourse (Neal 2004).

Women for Resurgence

Lastly, the future scenario for the Manipuri people in the tense, attritive challenge of the globalisation programme and the Look East Policy of the Indian state, cannot neglect what contribution the Manipuri women should make in evolving a 'national culture' to carry forward the civilizational struggle in the future. The present state of complete subjugation of Manipuri womanhood into servile social reproducers, the reduction of the market women into wage-earners, and general gender insensitivity and distorted cruelty over the body of Manipuri women reflect the heinous decline of the Manipuri civilization. For Manipuri civilization was based on the principle of women's basic role as the source of energy, of grace and of inclusivity. The principle of fertility which the ancients emphasized in food production and biological reproduction was intersticed into the concepts of polity functioning and social engineering processes of the past. Women were the subject of the culture's attention, that a simple look into the intricate marriage rituals would reveal how society cared for the 'woman', and that all activities in life, relationships and concerns were based on the basic acknowledgement of the importance of the 'woman'. All civilizational mores were built up in her care. She was not only the mother and the procreator, but also the polity organizer and cultural ambassador. She was the catalyst of the multi-ethnic social organism of the past, was the educator of values, of language and of societal networks of pluralism, that the basic structures of kin and blood ties were all built up on the body of the woman. The pre-colonial Manipur was a gendered polity. Women who acted as instruments of state in the international scenario, are still remembered in folk memory by extra-territorial ethnic neighbours. Princess Kuranganayani is remembered by the Ahoms, Princess Chandrapabha is still revered by the Dimasas of North Cachar Hills, and many other women had left their imprints for services to inter-ethnic harmony and polity equilibrium. These legacies are forgotten by present day 'feminists' and women's rights activists, as well as the general academia. The Meira-Paibees had become symbols of resistance against the repressive state, but their role and functions are still derided by partisan columnists of the national media, as well as the security forces who taunt them as 'Petticoat soldiers'. The resurgence of women are always a fact of Manipuri society's history, but the nature and direction of their struggle, the retrieval of their ancient civilizational heritage, and re-empowerment of their being in tune with current challenges to be faced are all imperatives for a whole generation of Manipuris to understand and acknowledge. The tragedy of Irom Sharmila reflects the general political apathy of the Manipuri people, the indifference to the sanctity of Manipuri women, and relentless insensitivity to their cause, whose predicament now reflect the depth of degeneration and decline of contemporary Manipuri culture and civilization. We Manipuris are not ourselves, we are others!

The re-opening of the Eastern Door should be challenged by the Manipuris, not in terms of simple acceptance of global processes which shall ride roughshod over the weak, indolent, and non-productive citizens, but as natural, empowered partners in the re-discovery and use of hitherto suppressed civilizational energy, now unleashed by contemporary challenger civilizations of East and Southeast Asia. The Mongoloid countries of East and Southeast Asia had now thrown up vital challenges to the economy and culture of other peoples, and other nations by the new discovery of their own tradition and heritage, their collective values, and their new Asian Affirmation (Huntington 1996). They have now emphasized that the nation should precede over the (ethnic) community and society over self; that Family should be the basic unit of society, that there should be Regard and Community Support for the Individual; that Consensus should be sought instead of contention; and that there should be Racial tolerance and religious harmony (White Paper of Singapore - President Wee Kim Wee 1991). What the East and South East Asian had emphasized in the context of globalisation is what is now termed as the 'Re-Asianization of Asia' (Aratalsozaki, 1992; Naff, 1984) as a post-imperial project. Taking similar queue from these cultural affines, the Manipuris should seriously undertake the project of 'Re-Manipurinization of Manipur' in the new era of globalisation.

REFERENCES

Aratalsozaki, 1992, Quoted by Huntington, Samuel 1996 , *Clash of Civilization and Remaking of the World Order,* Penguin Books, New Delhi.

Frank, 1969, *Latin America: Under development of Revolution,* Monthly Preview Press, New York.

Galtung, 1975, "A Structural Theory of Imperialism", *Journal of Peace Research*, Vol. 8.

Huntington, Samuel 1996, *Clash of Civilization and Remaking of the World Order,* Penguin Books, New Delhi.

Inkeles and Smith 1974, Quoted by Sijuwade, 2004.

Koves, M. 2004, "Fascism in the Age of Global Capitalism", *Social Scientist* - Sept-Oct. 2004.

Naff, W.E. 1985, Quoted by S. Huntington, *op cit.*.

Neal, Andrew W. 2004, Cutting off the King's Head - Foucault's Society must be defended and the problem of Sovereignty - Alternatives, New Delhi.

Ramesh, Jairam 2004, Speech at International Seminar organized by Centre for South East Asian Studies, OKD, Guwahati.

Robb, A. 2003, China's role in Burma, *Burma News*, June Vol. 14, No. 6, Peace Way Foundation, Bangkok.

Sijuwade, Philip O., 2004, 'Global Economy and Changes in the Determinants of Cross-National Income Equality'. *Journal of Indian School of Political Economy*, New Delhi.

4

Globalisation and Krishna Consciousness: An Overview

—AMAL SANASAM

Globalisation has been defined in two broad contexts, which are not very far from one another. One is the economic context, the other that of non-economic which broadly includes socio-cultural, historical and political dimensions of globalisation.

Although the economic argument behind globalisation appears stronger and widespread than other arguments, there is more than one economic interpretation. The European Commission has defined globalisation " as the process by which markets and productions in different countries are becoming increasingly interdependent due to the dynamics of trade in goods and services and flows of capital and technology".

The non-economic in general and the socio-cultural domain of globalisation in particular, appears more complex than its economic counterpart. Social analysis of globalisation is obviously a complex exercise in that it includes all aspects of human life of which economy is only a part, regardless of how important or fundamental this part may be. This also makes the social aspects of globalisation less tangible, and precise than its economic aspects in which the assessable units such as money and goods are by nature largely quantitative and more precise.

Nevertheless, sociologists are among the few of the social scientists who came out with a more precise definition of globalisation. Giddens, Robertson and Waters pioneered a specifically sociological definition of the concept notably at the time of its infancy. Giddens looked at globalisation as a consequence of the distinct sociological theme of modernity. Robertson emphasizes globalisation as a concept, which refers both to the compression of world and the intensification of consciousness of the world as a whole. For Waters globalisation is almost akin to centralization of social life.

According to K.K. Khuler in the modern context globalisation is a recent phenomenon, only about thirty years old. But, as concept and philosophy it is as old as the globe. In non-technical words globalisation means sharing, caring, partnership and togetherness. It rests on inter-dependence, mutuality and friendliness. In a global society often people sail and sink together. In fact globalisation transcends regional barriers and makes profound impact upon the people.

Historically speaking globalisation is an Indian concept. A hymn in the Vedas defines it as '*Vasudhaiv Kutumbkum*' meaning that 'the world is one family'. The old Tamil poem '*Kural*' by Thiru Valluvar refers to the whole world as a village. Swami Vivekananda's *Vedanta* is global in its content and core. The new world order which he visualized was based on the concept of '*Jiva is Shiva*" i.e. all human beings are equal and that a happy amalgam of the best of qualitative consciousness of the East and the West would make the world a better place to live and contemplate.

In our civilization and cultural context spiritual growth of the world is more important than the globalisation of economy. We do not know whether our culture is destined to play a significant role, in the modern times as it did with the past but we do understand that religious movement like 'Krishna Consciousness' is building up a new cultural ethos, which may ultimately bring peace to us and our society. It is in this context that I have selected my topic as "Globalisation and Krishna Consciousness: An overview."

In modern society the need of religion is no less paramount. As long as suffering exist in this world, the value and essence of religion is necessary. It is of course true that religion is sometimes too much associated with supernaturalism and dogmatism but the recent trends in religion have tended to place more emphasis in social values and less on dogma. This idea has become a global concept.

Evolutionist such as Tylor and Muller attempted to explain religion in terms of human needs. Tylor saw it as a response to man's intellectual needs, Muller saw it as a means for satisfying man's emotional needs. The functionalist perspective changes the emphasis from human needs to society's needs. Functionalists' analysis is primarily concern with the contribution religion makes to meeting the functional prerequisites or basic needs of society. From this perspective, the present Manipuri society requires a certain degree of social solidarity, value consensus and harmony and integration between its different parts. The role of International Society for Krishna Consciousness (ISKCON), Manipur is to bring these functional requisites or the basic needs of the society.

Krishna is one of the most popular Hindu Gods in the West. He is adored for his political acumen. He is universalized by the 'Krishna Consciousness Movement'. Established in 1965 in New York and better known as the 'Hare Krishna'. It is perhaps the first concept of globalizing the Indian culture in modern times. It has become a form of Global Hinduism. Global Hinduism contrast with Hindu nationalism. The former lays emphasis on what it perceives to be common spiritual values such as social justice and peace. It became important in the contemporary world because many elements of Hinduism have become widely available to those outside Hindu culture. It is felt in many societies that their social system has become too materialistic and individualistic. Perhaps these two factors are responsible for the many ills in their society. So they are looking for some tested formula for resolving the spiritual void and stabilizing human interpersonal relationships. ISKCON is stepping into this void and providing the emotional security within academic exercise- which is the food for mind. Once the physical needs are fulfilled man needs food for thought to keep his mind active as well as balanced. Spiritualism therefore is the need of the hour.

The impact of globalisation in Manipur in the realm of religion is on account of the existence of Vaishnavism as a 'Cult'. It is a well-known fact that the influence or the religious movement of Vaisnavas culture started in the 18th cent. In this light Swami Prabhupada, the founder Acharya of the ISKCON was familiar with the rich Vaisnava heritage of Manipur. He desired to preserve this Manipuri Vaishnava culture and to show the world the example of an ideal Vaishnava state. He instructed his desciple, T. Damudor, a native of Manipur, to revive the Vaishnava culture of Manipur.

Thus the advent of ISKCON has revived Manipuri Vaishnava culture, as well as the emergence of Krishna Consciousness among the minds of the people. Ever since it started during the time of king Bhagyachandra. He had seen a vision- Krishna riding an elephant, coming to his help in Assam when he had to tame a wild elephant in front of the king and people of Assam to establish his identity as the genuine Bhagychandra. It had a great impact upon our society. Idols of Lord Krishna were made and established in different parts of Manipur. The statue of Krishna, which was selected by the king as per his vision, was called Govindaji. This idol was made from the wood of jackfruit trees. He also started a new dance form- Rasa Lila to be performed especially for the God Krishna and his consort Radha Rani. Rasa Lila and Krishna Consciousness was revived as ISKCON movement, the people found a place in the movement itself. The culture and civilization of Manipur is pervaded with Krishna Consciousness.

The people have become Vaishnavas, devotees of Krishna. But they express their devotion with a special Manipuri spirit. We know that religion is a part of cultural system, religious beliefs give meaning to life, they answer mans' questions about himself, his values and the world we live in.

In order to preserve and revive earnestly this culture several steps have been taken—first, T. Damudor started the ISKCON temple in Manipur in Dec. 25ft, 1977. ISKCON Manipur has now completed 25 yrs dedicated service to this mission. Second, Bhaktivedanta Institute Mission School in Imphal (1979) and Moirang (1987), third Ranganiketan- a

Manipuri Cultural Arts troupe promoting Manipuri traditional Vaishnava culture around the world was initiated in 1989. Further a Nature Cure hospital and a Yogic Ashram was established in 1995, and has also started the university of Bhagavata culture. He organized socially relevant seminars, peace marches, and conferences and contributed significantly towards peace in Manipur and around the world. He has created a niche for himself. A socio-religious and cultural movement is thus afoot. Academician and man with broader academic horizon have joint it. They have become part and parcel of this movement. So, in the process of globalisation for peace initiative Manipur is not lagging behind. The need is to understand the importance of peace initiatives and our positive response to it.

Manipur is a small state. People are by and large superficially contended. Economic improvements are taking place. New markets are coming up under the stress of global capital. So it can act as a model state. We know that social, political, economic and religious churning in the minds of intellectuals is taking place and more among the common people. So we can think of evolving a model of peace, which may become acceptable globally and show a path of peace and progress for the global society instead of perpetuating the gun culture, which is searing the society. It is in this connection that as early as June 2000 ISKCON took a lead by forming a United Religious Initiative at Pittsburgh. The preamble States:

> We, people of diverse religions,
> Spiritual expressions and indigenous
> Traditions throughout the world, hereby establish
> the United Religions Initiative to
> Promote enduring, daily interfaith cooperation,
> to end Religiously motivated violence
> And to create cultures of peace, justice and healing
> For the Earth and all living beings.

So Manipur's idea of peace was acceptable to many countries (77). This was to end the culture of violence and bring peace and happiness globally.

CONCLUSION

As a sociologist I feel that there is a reverse process for globalisation in which regional, local, groups or ethnic communities can come out with their ideas for maintaining peace like the streams or rivers which originate at different places yet meet at the sea, where it becomes very vast and deep. Maintaining global peace is difficult for global terrorism. Cultural emphasis in social settings is needed. Social deprivation must be addressed to. The people will have to rise above parochial considerations in order to realize their common dream.

REFERENCES

Economic and Political Weekly, August 18th, 2001.

Haralambros, M. and R.H Heald, (1989), *Sociology: Themes and Perspectives*.

Hood, Gavin, *Indian Religions & the Hindu Tradition, Cambridge Illustrated History of Religions*. Edited by John Bowler.

Khullar, K.K., (2005), "Globalisation & India", *Employment News*, 29 Jan-4 Feb., 2005.

Madan, T.N., *Religion of Indian Plurality and Pluralism*. The Oxford India Companion to Sociology and Social Anthropology. Edited by Veena Das.

Singh, E. Nilakanta, (1993), *Fragments of Manipuri Culture*.

Singh, I. M., *My Search for God*.

Singh, Yogendra, (2000), *Cultural Change in India: Identity and Globalisation*.

The University of Bhagavata Culture, (2002), *A Glimpse of 25 Years of ISKON in Manipur*, Imphal.

Zaidiman, Nurit, "American ISKON Temple", *The Eastern Anthropologist*, Vol. 49: No. 3-4.

5

Cultural Interaction and Growth: A Case Study of Leimaram, a Scheduled Caste Village of Manipur

—W. NABAKUMAR

[ABSTRACT

The inhabitants of Leimaram village, who bear the popular ethnonyme of Chakpa Leimarams, are a little known Scheduled Caste Community also a constituent group of the larger Loi people of Manipur who occupied a lower social status in the social hierarchy of the Meitei society because of their engagement, during the historical days, in the callings denied to the Meiteis and assimilated themselves, at different periods of historical past, into the sociocultural fabric of their reference group, the Meiteis, by way of adopting the lifeways of the later. The paper devotes to the explanation of change and continuity in the socio-cultural life of the people in order to elucidate one of the seeming paradoxes of culture, that is, culture is both static and dynamic in the light of the surface appearance of the change the people have experienced because of their voluntary conversion into Hinduism on one hand and the folk cultural elements and meaning still present in the cultural life of the people either in their original or socially metamorphosed form on the other.]

I

The subject matter of the paper calls for a brief introduction on the place - name, Leimaram and its inhabitants, who prefer to call themselves as Chakpas, though the name is not yet recognized by the administration, for the explanation of the same theoretically centres around the village and its people. Leimaram is a Scheduled Caste village situated at a distance of about 25 km to the southwest of Imphal, the metropolitan, capital-town of Manipur. From Imphal the State Highway-Tiddim Road runs southwestward leading to Moirang, a localised place of the distressful, legendary love story of Khamba and Thoibi that still remains alive in every Meitei's heart of heart and the greatest hill town Churachandpur, the headquarters of Churachandpur District, the native place of various Kuki-Chin speaking tribes of Manipur. If somebody travels from Imphal by bus along the road, he will see through the windows of the bus a number of small bazars, clustered villages, small hillocks situated by the side of the road, sometimes the vast expanse of meadows and fields stretching far and wide beyond the limit of his vision and also isolated small villages, that seem to be small groves being far off from the road. After travelling for about twenty km. he comes across a small hill, called Lokpaching which, standing majestically beside the road, over looks all passer-by. After a short distance of about a quarter of a km from there to the south, a metalled road bifurcates from the Tiddim Road and runs westward in twists and turns through the vast paddy fields which extend far afield on all sides. The meandering road, after crossing the paddy field, touches a small Meitei village, called, Heinoubok, on the west of which there lies the village, Leimaram inhabited by the Chakpas, a Scheduled Caste community of Manipur. The road, after running through the heart of Heinoubok village, suddenly twists northward and again westward, and physically separates the village Leimaram from the former village. After running a short winding course, the road runs straight through the interior of the village, Leimaram and finally reaches its destination when it touches the mountain ranges located on the western side of the village, Leimaram.

The village Leimaram, sharing a common boundary with the Meitei village Heinoubok on the east, is fronted by the Meiteis and blocked on the west by high mountain ranges inhabited by tribes like the Koms, the Kabuis etc. and moreover surrounded on the north and the south by the vast stretch of paddy field and meadows. It falls within the administrative jurisdiction of Bishenpur District. The village is well communicated with the surrounding Meitei villages, like Kabowakching, Kangmong, Irengbam, Maibam etc. by a network of roads.

The village slopes down to the east as it is situated at the foot of mountain ranges. It is very rich in vegetation and has a settlement area of about 994.84 acres which comprises residential site, cultivable land, meadows, reserved forest and playground. Every household, which generally consists of two or three houses, sometimes more, is physically demarcated from neighbouring ones by mud walls covered with thick vegetation, and a trench dug all round. Sometimes two or more households generally established by married brothers have such a demarcation. The houses of the village range from traditional houses made of bamboo and roofed over with thatch, through houses with wooden structures and corrugated iron sheet roof, to modern style, brick and cement structures of one or two stories, though the number of the latter is very few. Every household generally consists of one residential house or more if needed and two or more huts or buildings meant for different purposes, such as storage of agricultural produce, firewood and so on. A separated cow-shed is a must for every household as the economy of the village centres around agriculture. On the whole, the village, though it is a Scheduled Caste village, has a prosperous look and is on a par in all respects with the surrounding Meitei villages.

II

The people of Leimaram village, locally known as the Chakpa Leimarams, are a constituent group of the larger Loi community of Manipur. The Lois, from the historical perspective, were a group of people who paid tribute to the king or who were ostracised to Loi villages for violating cultural conventions and consequently degraded to Lois. The former comprised a number of occupational groups, such as silk manufactures, iron smelters, potters, salt manufactures, fishers, post and beam cutters, canoe makers, and payers of 'Sel', the coin. Of the Lois of Manipur, the 'Sel Loi', was considered the lowest (McCulloch. 1857). A person became a Loi either by birth or by a royal decree of punishment. In case of the latter the person concerned could be forgiven after a while and could be remitted, otherwise his family and descendants became Loi. Thus, during the historical days, when Manipur was under the rule of autocratic kings, degradation of a person to the status of a Loi was regarded as the most severe from of punishment. Khangemba, who ruled Manipur in the year 1645 A.D. was the first Meitei king, who made deportation of grave offenders to Loi villages. (Hudson 1908: 9). He further documented that Garibnewas (1709-1748), who brought religious changes in the state, made wholesale deportation of his subjects, specially those who opposed him, to Loi villages.

Hudson was of the opinion that Lois of different villages were of different origins. He mentioned that Sekmai Lois were said to have moved there from the south whereas Fayeng and Andro Lois once occupied the site of Konung or fort from where they were driven out by Pakhangba. According to him the Kakching Lois, who lived by iron smelting, were once under the rule of Heirok king and the Loi villages such as Thanga, Ithing, and Sugnu were penal settlements, to which all classes of offenders were sent. "The original rearers of silk worm came from Kabo, from whence they appear to have brought the worm" (McCulloch: 1857:33)

The Lois, in its historical specific connotation, thus include those people, who occupied the lowest stratum in the traditional social hierarchy of the Meitei society because of their engagements in the different occupational callings which were, both theoretically and practically, denied to the Meiteis. During monarchial regime of Meitei kings, they paid tribute in goods, whose manufacturer was solely in their hands, to the kings. In the historical past, the different Loi people who monopolised the manufacturer of different goods, were exempted from Lalup, which was a form of force labour and a must for the Pana Meiteis. As the Pana system of the Meitei did not embrace the Lois, the former kept the latter outside the social framework of their society. This dialectical distinction became more distinct when Garibnewas introduced Vaishnavism as the state religion because the Loi communities were not allowed to embrace Vaishnavism as their religion. It is, however, necessary to underline the fact that in the historical process of nation building of the Meiteis many of the Lois embraced Vaishnavism and identified themselves with the former by way of giving up their traditional callings and imitating the way of life of their reference community at the expense of their traditional rituals and conventions considered inferior by the latter.

The contextual specific connotation of the term "Loi" is found to be different from its historical specific connotation. In its present context and meaning it embraces only the Lois who have been enlisted in the list of Scheduled Caste. Thus, the term, in its current sense, does not cover many of the Lois who were regarded as Lois in the historical past. The meaning of the term has reoriented to such as an extent that it means Schedule Caste to the ordinary layman. Many of the Loi communities, as started earlier, ceased to be Loi by adopting Vaishnavism as their religion. Consequently, the term Loi seems to cover only those Loi communities enlisted in the Scheduled list.

The Chikpa Leimarams are said, as documented in their folk history, to have had a common origin with the Fayeng and Andro Lois. They, being a Loi community, paid tribute to the kings, who ruled over Manipur during different historical periods. During the monarchial regime of the Meitei kings, they had to pay a quantum of silk thread for the purpose of garments for the royal family. According to the name of material they paid as tribute, they were also known as *Kabrang Kisi Loi (Kabrang*=silk; *Kisi*=knot; *Loi*= the root of the word *Loiba* means to make or to finish). The term literally connotes the makers of silk thread. On Vaishnavism becoming the state religion, they, perhaps, were not expressly allowed to submit themselves to the norms expected of proselytes into Vaishnavism. Instead of acquiescing themselves in the norm of Vaishnavism, they rather continued to follow their traditional customs and practices. They were, thus, automatically placed in the lowest stratum of the Meitei social hierarchy.

This little known community has experienced a vigorous process of acculturation and many of its traditional customs and practices have been Sanskritised owing to its voluntary acceptance of Vaishnavism. They have claimed themselves to be Vaishnavite Hindus and engaged a Brahmin priest to officiate their ritual and religious ceremonies. They keep a Brahmin family, as other neighbouring villages do, to run a temple, where a number of Hindu gods and goddesses are being worshipped. Of late a contra-acculturative movement has gained momentum as there is growing consciousness of the indigenous identity among the people.

III

An introductory discussion on some theoretical concepts such as Sanskritisation and great and little tradition, which are found useful in the analysis of the cultural life of the Chakpa Leimarams, is being made in order to have a theoretical insight into the kind of socio-cultural changes experienced by the people under study. Sanskritisation is the academic trademark of M.N. Srinivas, who first used the term in his study of the Coorgs of South India with a view to describing the process of upward mobility of lower caste people in the caste hierarchy by adopting vegetarianism and teetotalism at the expense of their own traditional way of life considered impure by higher caste. (Srinivas: 1952: 32). As the concept was found theoretically fruitful in the study of tribal and village communities in different parts of India, Srinivas (1962; 1966) did vigorous academic exercise in his attempt to make theoretical refinement of the concept. "Sanskritisation means not only the adoption of new customs and habits but also exposure to new ideas and values, which have found frequent expression in the vast body of Sanskritic literature – sacred as well as secular" (Srinivas 1962: 48). He also broadened the academic connotation of the term and wrote: "Sanskritisation is a process by which a low Hindu caste, or tribal changes its customs, ritual and way of life in the direction of frequently twice born caste. Generally such changes are followed by a claim to a higher position in the caste hierarchy than that traditionally conceded to the claimant caste by the local community (Srinivas, 1966: 6). Though Sanskritisation suffers from theoretical looseness and academic vagueness (Harper, 1959, Stall, 1963; Singh, 1977) it has its own merits in describing the process of change in terms of culture but not in terms of structure.

The conceptual framework of great and little traditions for the study of social change was first postulated by Redfield (1956) in his study of Mexican communities. This approach, whose basic principles are "civilization" and "social organisation of tradition", is basically built on the view point of growing a civilization through orthogenetic or indigenous evolution as well as through heterogenetic contacts with other civilization. It also recognises the operation of social structure of this civilization at two different levels: one, that of the folk or unlettered peasants, and the other, that of the reflective few or the elite. Little tradition refers to the cultural processes of the former and great tradition comprises the later. "Indigenous civilization" and "secondary civilization" is resulted from the local folk cultures and societies, which have some foreign elements but without loss of their moral and cultural integration. A "secondary civilization" as represented in the theoretical scheme, is the modern, urban, western civilization and is the result of rapid development of technical order or growing increase in contact and communication with others or of both conditions. A civilization does not restrict to any particular kind of community, form of social relations, social class or kind of cultural product or capacity, such as writing. It rather connotes the total structure of communities - folk, present and urban - and the network of social relations which bind these communities together with a particular civilization, its social structure. Redfield handled the delimitation, identity and continuity of a civilization in terms of its" cultural structure", which comprises the structure of its cultural traditions and thought a values. This cultural structure, which is the resultant of the mutual interaction of "great" and "little" dimensions, is organised and transmitted through a specific "organisation of tradition". The cultural structure is thus complementary to its "societal structure". The whole "societal structure" of social networks and centres gets an obvious identity from the cultural content which consists of the systems of thoughts and values, that circulate through it. These systems of thoughts and values have local names and habitations given by the "cultural structure." The extent of a civilization is, thus, measured by the extent of cultural structure, but not by the spread of cultural traits.

McKim Marriott, using the conceptual tool developed by Redifield, conducted a study on the interaction of great and little traditions in Kishan Garhi, a village in U.P., India. He wrote, "concept of primary civilization type of process is one of the most inviting of available models for conceptualising Kishan Garhi's relations with its universe" (Marriott, 1955: 181). He recorded accretion of Sanskritic elements to the non-Sanskritic culture forms of the village than replacement of the latter by the former.

He analysed the constant interaction of great and little traditional elements with the conceptual framework of "Universalisation of little tradition" and "Parochialistion of great tradition". By former he meant the process of the interpretations and identification of elements of little tradition, indigenous customs and practices and local deities in terms of great tradition by bringing them up to the level of the latter. In the process the elements of little tradition may undergo cultural metamorphosis so that it may become an organic part of great tradition. By the latter concept he meant the specific process of circulating downward the elements of great tradition to the level of little tradition and identifying them with the legitimate form of the later.

IV

In the light of the above-discussed theoretical understanding an attempt has been made to analyse the cultural life of the Chakpa Leimarams particularly in respect of their pre- and post-Hindu *rites - de passage* and cyclic rituals and festivals with a view to giving a general picture of the contemporary culture of the people. In the pre-Hindu period the birth of a child is followed by the performance of a number of rituals for the welfare and longevity of the life of the child. Mention may be made of *Yupan thaba* ceremony, celebrated on the morning of the fifth or the sixth day after birth according to the six of the child by a local priestess, *Maibi, Cha-umba,* another ceremony celebrated on an auspicious day when the child was three months old and *nahutf-nareng tamba* (ear-lobe boring ceremony), a community ceremony celebrated collectively once in a year for all children who attained three years of age to signify the transition of the children from the grade of god to the grade of human beings. The ceremony was performed at the residence of the oldest boy of all children whose ear-lob boring ceremony was going to be celebrated on the same day and occasion. The title *nachingba* was given to the oldest boy. A girl was not entitled to get the title.

After the voluntary acceptance of Vaishnavite Hinduism many a change, sometimes replacement of the indigenous rituals by new Sanskritic rituals, has taken place, *Yupanthaba* is no longer performed at present as it has been replaced by a new one known as *Swastipujah,* celebrated on the six day of the birth irrespective of the sex of the child by a Brahmin priest with the recitation of Sanskritic *mantras.* Though *Cha-umba* (first taking of solid food) ceremony is still performed many changes have been occurred in the process of carrying out the ceremony. Nowadays it is celebrated when the child is six months old and custom of putting a black thread around the neck of the child to entrap its soul is no longer in vogue. Ear-lobe boring ceremony is also no more a community ceremony. Consequently the practice of selecting a *nachingba* has become obsolete.

The new faith-Hinduism has also brought about many changes in the marriage rituals as well as the outlook of the people as to the concept of marriage. Today among the Vaishnavite Chakpa Leimarams the loan Sanskritic word *Kanya dan* (rite of the gift of the virgin bride) is widely used in connection with a daughter's marriage. In the pre-Hindu days, no ritual ceremony was observed in connection with the marriage-by-elopement. A ceremony called *Loukhatpa* or *Khungatpa* was performed by the parents of the woman on the request of the parents of the man in order to give socially approved formal recognition to the marriage. The custom of bride service was prevalent in the pre-Hindu period and the period of bride service during which the married couple used to live at the natal home of the bride was known as *ya-ong inba*. At present the term denotes the cultural practice of living by the married couple at the residence of the bride if they wish and thus carries the meaning of matrilocal residence. Every married woman, according to the pre-Hindu cultural convention, had to offer a feast, called, *Khomin* (price of breast milk) to her parents in order to make herself free from the moral dept of bringing her up. At present *Khomim*, though not obsolete, is not obligatory on the part of a married woman. As they have adopted vegetarianism and teetotalism, meat and wine, the chief items of the pre-Hindu rituals, have been replaced by fish and water and a Brahmin priest officiates all the rituals.

The exposure of the Chakpa Leimarams to the idea of Sanskritic theology and literature, resulted from the voluntary adoption of Hinduism, has also resulted in changes occurred in the traditional mortuary rituals performed following the death of a person. *Papa, Karama, dharma, maya* and *sansara* have entered the day-to-day vocabulary of the people. A traditional ritual, *Chuksa moithemba,* by name, performed following an unnatural death of a person to prevent the recurrence of the same in the family and lineage of which the deceased was a member, is still performed with some modifications and replacements in the items of offerings when an unnatural death occurs in a family. However, *lukhunba,* the ritual of collecting half calcined bones in an unfired earthen pot by old men and women when the cremation is over and *luphu phumba,* the ritual of burying that pot after proper decoration according to the sex of the deceased are no longer performed at present. The last mortuary ritual of the pre-Hindu days was *mathouyangemba,* performed on a day of *Wakching* and *Phairen* as fixed by *Khunlakpa* of the village, in commemoration of the dead person. At present this has been replaced by a ceremony, called, *phiroy* performed on the first death anniversary of the deceased.

The Chakpa-Leimarams, in their pre-Hindu days, performed a number of cyclic rituals and festivals both on the household and community levels with a view to promoting their over all welfare. *Shajibu Lakyel Taiba Kum on Kishinaiba* was a ritual ceremony performed on the first day of *Shajibu,* the first month of the local calendar year, by every household in ritual honour of household god, *Sanamahi,* and goddess, *Leimaran,* who ritually preside over every household of pre-Hindu Chakpa of Leimaram. At present, it is known as Cheiraoba and performed on a certain day of *Sajibu,* but not on the first day.

Kurak lamdaiba is another pre-Hindu ritual which is still performed without much significant change though performed in a somewhat abbreviated form because of the obsolescence of the enlistment of *shois,* bachelor-members who belong to a particular age-grade. Even dogs and fowls are sacrificed to the deity in whose honour the ritual is performed though blood sacrifice is strictly prohibited by the new religion.

Langban Kumeiba, a big feast arranged by the members of a concerned lineage on a day of the first fortnight of *Langban,* the six month of the year, for the overall integration and solidarity of the concerned lineage is still performed by the villagers with some alterations in the menu of the feast.

In the pre-Hindu days a ritual - *Ashimal thaba* - was performed on a day of the second fortnight of *Langban* in order to get divine protection from the deceased ancestors by the male head of every household. At present it is known as *Langban Tarapan* and the offering of meal to the soul of the deceased forefathers is performed by a Brahamin in a feast at which members of the concerned lineage, relatives and friends are also entertained. The whole period of the second fortnight of *Langban* is now regarded as a period of propitiation of deceased ancestors and a ritual is performed on the morning of all days of this period by offering fruits and flowers to the soul of the deceased forefathers in a pond or a running stream, which is being regarded as one of the forms of the holy Ganges.

Another ritual ceremony performed both in the pre-Hindu and post-Hindu periods without much significant change is *Singja Pokpi Khurumba,* celebrated in the month of *Langban,* in ritual honour of the village deity and his wife in order to seek divine omens from the deity about the happening of the year to come. The whole ritual complex consists of a number of rituals like inviting the deity to the ritual and offering of cooked food and liquor. No significant change is evident in the process of performing these rituals, which constitute the ritual complex, but substitution of fish carry and water for meat curry and liquor is noticed under the impact of Hinduism.

Lamta, the last month of the year is a ritually important month, for different rituals are performed in this month. Among the traditional rituals, which are still being performed without any change, *Khunthong Lakpa, Saroi Khangba* and *Apumbi Khurumba* may be mentioned. *Khunthong Laikpa* is performed on the first Saturday of *Lamta* by menfolk of the village in order to protect the village from the evil spirits, who are believed to come down from the heaven to the earth in the month of *Lamta* and enter the village through the four gates of four directions. It is performed to appease four gods, who ritually preside over four directions, by offering fowls, fish etc, which, by the standard of the new religion, are considered impure. *Saroi khangba,* which shares some motive and significance with *Khunthonglakpa,* is performed by womenfolk of the village on all Saturdays of *Lamta* except the first one to appease the evil spirits, who are supposed to be the cause of worldly sufferings. *Apumbi Khurumba* is also performed by the womenfolk on an auspicious day of *Lamta* to please the spirits of the children who died before attaining three years of age and at the same time to prevent the recurrence of such unfortunate incidents.

Lai-Haraoba, a complex whole of rituals and festivals performed in honour of the village deity and his wife, is another traditional ritual cum festival still performed by the villagers, though it suffers a little change from the impact of Hinduism, with traditional fervour and enthusiasm. As found in other Sanskritised rituals, the replacement of liquor by water and meat curry by fish curry by fish curry is found in the rituals of *Lai-Haraoba.* In the past a community hunt was performed and the animal killed or captured was sacrificed to the father-god and mother-goddess. Such a community hunt is no longer performed at present as animal sacrifice is forbidden by the new religion. Over and above the aforementioned rituals and festivals, the Chakpa Leimarams have also directly or indirectly participated in a number of Hindu festivals celebrated by the Vaishnavite Meiteis and celebrated non-cyclic Hindu festivals like *Ras-Leela* and *Goura-Leela*.

V

It is now evident on evaluation that the Chakpa Leimarams, by voluntarily converting themselves into Hinduism, have adopted a number of Sanskritic crises rituals at the expense of their traditional folk rituals with a view to pushing up their social status in the social milieu of Meitei society. Some of the traditional crises ritual practices had been culturally discarded through a process, what Srinivas called Sanskritisation. It is also, however, found that in case of some rituals, instead of making total replacement by Sanskritic rituals, the folk elements to form a remade new ritual whole. Thus instances of the universalization of little tradition rather than Sanskritisation are also noticed in the process of interaction of the two traditions. Moreover, some of the traditional cyclic rituals, though some of their folk elements are not usually acceptable to the new religion, are still being performed without bringing about much change. To the Chakpa Leimarams, Hinduism is not a total substitution for their traditional folk religion. Despite their claim of being Hindus by religion they do not totally give up their traditional beliefs; they instead have either adopted Sanskritic rituals or brought forward the traditional rituals, which have affinity with the Sanskritic rituals, to the level of Sanskritic tradition in order to identify them as Sanskritic ones. The universalization of some folk elements is made in such a manner that only a deep prove and analysis reveal the presence of folk elements in the universalized rituals. No doubt, there are also rituals in which folk elements overshadow Sanskritic elements. In such rituals only the items of materials, which are ritually considered impure or unclean, have been replaced, without any change in the process of performing the rituals, buy ritually clean, Sanskritic materials. Three grades of rituals– the purely Sanskritic rituals, the rituals which contain both traditional and Sanskritic elements at varying degrees and the purely traditional rituals constitute the local Hinduism professed by the Chakpa Leimarams.

REFERENCES

Harper, E.B., (1959), "A Hindu Village Pantheon", *South Western Journals of Anthropology*, Vol. XV: 227-234.

Hudson T.C., (1908), *The Meiteis,* Delhi, B.R. Publishing Corp.

Marriott, Mc-Kim (ed), (1955), *Village India,* Chicago, University of Chicago Press.

McCulloch M., (1857). *Account of the Valley of Manipur,* Delhi, Gian Publications.

Redfield, R., (1934), "Cultural Change in Yukatan", *American Anthropologists* 36: 57-69

Redfield, R., 1955(56), "The Social Organisation of Tradition", *Far Eastern Quarterly,* 15.

Redfield, R., (1956), *Peasant Society and Culture: An Anthropological Approach to Civilization,* Chicago, Chicago University Press.

Singh, Yogendra, (1977), *Modernisation of Indian Tradition*, Faridabad, Thomson Press (India) Ltd.

Srinivas, M.N., (1952), *Religion and Society Among the Coorgs of South India,* Oxford, Clarendon Press.

Srinivas, M.N., (1962), *Caste in Modern India and Other Essays,* Bombay, Asia Publishing House.

6

Place in a Placeless World: Nationalism and Globalisation in Manipur

—KONJENGBAM MEGHACHANDRA SINGH

[ABSTRACT

The new communications technologies that developed in the second half of the twentieth century have reduced the significance of time and space. Nation states are no longer significant actors or meaningful economic units in many ways. Consumer tastes and cultures are homogenized and satisfied through provision of standardized global products created by global corporates with no allegiance to place or community. However movements for nationalism and sub-nationalism prevail across the world. This paper makes an attempt to analyse some aspects of nationalism in the age of globalisation in the context of Manipur.]

Globalisation or Time-Space Compression

As a concept, globalisation emerged around 1960 when the Canadian media scholar Marshall McLuhan coined the term *global village* to capture the impact of new communications technologies on social and cultural life.[1] The consequent time-space compression has transformed the structure and scale of human relationships that social, cultural, political and economic processes now operate at a global scale with a consequent reduction in the significance of other geographical scales (national, local, etc.). Importance of nation states as significant actors or meaningful economic actors has reduced whereas consumer tastes and cultures are homogenized and satisfied through provision of standardized global products created by global corporate with no allegiance to place or community. Writers such as Kenichi Ohmae[2] speak of a borderless world in which the nation-state has become rendered impotent by institutions, including multi-national corporations, which operate globally and without any economic openness, economic interdependence and deepening economic integration between countries. Economic openness, interdependence and integration may be in terms of trade flows, investment flows, flows of services, technologies, information and ideas. Economic interdependence is, however, highly asymmetrical. There is high degree of interdependence among the developed countries and a considerable dependence of the developing countries on the developed countries.

The social dimension of globalisation is that the creation of a market society usually leads to the pursuit of material well-being as an exclusive objective. Material culture may distort or even uproot norms and values which form the very foundation of the society. Thus, social institutions, so essential for the market economy itself can be progressively weakened.

Considering the cultural dimension of globalisation, the term connotes "the increasing world-wide sharing of symbols and the awareness of a global social entity."[4] The information and communication technology revolution has made possible the global spread of cultural impulses. Erla Zwingle[5] elaborated the flow of culture from the West to the East and vice versa. Even the cultures of the East such as applying henna paste are quite common in the West. To some writer the processes of globalisation are perceived to be a threat to culture in the sense that market opportunity rather than national identity functions as the new reality of international media operations.[6] To them global integration provokes national disintegration as ethnic, cultural or religious passions fragment society. However, many scholars are abandoning both nostalgic worries about the loss of local culture and the enthusiastic celebration of post-modern tolerance, to focus instead on local interpretation of the heterogeneous input received through the market.[7]

Politically, the most important aspect of globalisation is the much contested concept of 'hallowing out' of the nation-state. For the momentum of globalisation, national governments have to be reduced and incursions are to be made into the sovereign political space. However this is not always accompanied by a corresponding increase in international cooperation.

Place in a Placeless World

Globalisation, as seen from the above discussion, dilutes geographical and political boundaries, cultural identities, social norms, values, practices and institutions of people who inhabit geographical spaces. The global is , thus, claimed to be the natural order of affairs in today's technologically driven world in which time – space has been compressed , the 'end of geography' has arrived and everywhere is becoming the same.[8] This is referred to as the placeless-ness of the world. And in the placeless world, the view of globalisation as an inexorable, and virtually unstoppable, force which can only be accommodated, rather than resisted, has become the conventional wisdom in neo-liberal political and economic circles and even employed by some powerful nations as a rhetoric to justify hegemonic political decisions. When the significance of place or territory is reduced and when cultural identity is diluted by market driven forces of globalisation, how can the assertion of space and identity, as manifested in nationalism and sub-nationalism particularly in the North-Eastern region of India, be located? How will globalisation encounter these 'national' and 'sub-national' movements? Attempt can be made here to address these questions in the context of Manipur.

Becoming Placeless

Politically, globalisation refers to the increasing importance of worldwide governance regimes, not exclusively but largely based again on the state system.[9] Creation of macro-regions such as EU, SAARC, NATO, etc. as regulatory powers of nation-states, thus, becomes significant. This follows the agreement between nation-states. History has told us that emerging world orders produce new alliances. The break up of the Soviet Union, the emergence of a unipolar world after the end of cold war and new developments in the bilateral relation with China, among others, prompt India to venture for the "Look-East" policy. This is with the objective of a greater regional cooperation with the South-East Asia. Thus geographical and political barriers of the North-East will be made less significant to accommodate flow of people, goods, knowledge and technology between India and South-East Asia. This development towards placeless-ness can be observed in the backdrop of nationalism and sub-nationalism in Manipur.

In Manipur, many outfits are demanding either complete secession or autonomy of 'territories' that they claim to be theirs. The floating of Hindu Army by members of Bengali, Nepali, Marwari, Punjabi, Tamil and Bihari communities with active patronage from the National Socialist Council of Nagalism (NSCN-IM) and the United Kuki Liberation Front (UKLF) of Manipur has added one more outfit to the already existing twenty-three outfits, nine in the valley and fourteen in the hills currently operating in the state of Manipur. (*The Telegraph*, June18, 2003, Guwahati; as quoted in Koireng).[10] The assertion of space (cf. territory) and identity by these numerous outfits, in certain cases, led to even ethnic cleansing in the state. In Manipur, the 1990s was best remembered for the row of violent ethnic clashes that arose out of the exclusivist agenda and expansionist design of the different ethnic armies complemented by the mutual antagonism on competing interests.[11] The Kuki-Naga clash started in 1992 and continued unabated till 1997. The Meitei and Muslim Clash in May 1993 was "contained within a week as it was not a communal riot though it took an inter-denominational colour".[12] Latest in the chain of ethnic clashes in the state was the Kuki-Paite Clash. Thus while globalisation reduces the significance of 'place', secessionist movements asserts it.

Globalisation Vs Nationalism

These two processes are at interplay in Manipur. However while globalisation is having a joyride, nationalism is facing a number of obstacles that globalisation does not come across. These obstacles are:

1. Inter-outfit conflict/clash among outfits.
2. Factional rivalry within outfits.
3. Cultural imperialism as patroned by globalisation itself.

The list is not exhaustive. However the interplay between the two processes is not assessed yet. Thus the unprecedented urbanization in Imphal city, which is by and large the impact of globalisation, is underscored and the concentration of affluent representations of each community in the capital is ignored. And the secessionist outfits of the hills explain the process in terms of hill-valley dichotomy or Meitei hegemonism rather than a rural-urban dichotomy. It should be noted here that about ten percent of the total population of the state is in less than 0.1 percent of the total area of the state (in Imphal city). And more than two-third of the population is in less than one-tenth of the total area of the state (in the valley districts).[13] And the valley districts, particularly Imphal districts, have acquired the cosmopolitan feature with sizable population of different ethnic groups in the state. This urban-centric population concentration is associated with urban amenities, which are in fact the agents of globalisation. The question will remain as to which one will have a greater momentum-placeness or placelessness.

NOTES

1. Johnston, R.J. *et al.*, (2000). *The Dictionary of Human Geography*. Oxford: Blackwell Publishers Ltd. pp.315.
2. Ohmae, Kenichi (1990). *The Borderless World: Power and Strategy in The Interlinked Economy*. New York: The Free Press.
3. Newman, David and Nurit Kliot (2000), 'Introduction: Globalisation and the Changing World Political Map'. In: Nurit Kliot and David Newman (eds.), *Geopolitics at the End of the Twentieth Century,* London: Frank Cass. pp. 1-2
4. Wusten, H. van der (1998), Globalisation and Geography: editorial. *Geojournal.* 45(1-2): 1.

5. Zwingle, Evla (1999), Goods move. People move. Ideas move. and Cultures Change. *National Geographic,* August 1999.
6. Morley, D. and K. Robins (1995), *Spaces of Identity.* London: Routledge.
7. Conti, S. and P. Giaccaria (1998), Globalisation: A Geographical Discourse. *Geojournal.* 45(12): 17.
8. Johnston, R. J. *et al., op. cit.,* p. 315.
9. Wusten, H. van der. *op. cit.,* p. 1.
10. Koireng, Aheibam. Growth of Sub-Nationalism and Displacement in the North-East India with Special Reference to Manipur. Paper presented at the National Seminar on *Problems of Governance and State of Human Rights in North-East India,* organized by Dept. of Pol. Sc., Dibrugarh University. P. 4.
11. *Ibid.,* p. 4.
12. Quoted in Koireng, Aheibam. *Ibid.,* p.4.
13. *Census of India, 2001.* Primary Census Abstract.

7

Colonialism, Culturocide and Denial of Shared History: An Experience in Manipur Hills

—AHEIBAM KOIRENG SINGH

Introduction

The British colonization of Manipur was complete with the defeat of Manipur at the Anglo-Manipur War of 1891. Consequently, the British Political Agent exercised considerable influence particularly in the matter of administration of tribal areas. While the Maharaja and the Manipur state Darbar were permitted to administer the Hindu Meitei populated Manipur valley, the hill tribes were administered by the British political agent. The political agent who was already burdened with the Presidentship of the Manipur State durbar carried out the hill administration through some petty officials, *lambu*. When Pettigrew came to Manipur for spreading Christianity, the British did not allow Christianity propagation of the new faith in the valley by the Political Agent. Instead, they were allowed to carry on their mission work and propagation in the hills of Manipur. Thus the Manipur hills, for the first time, came into contact with the western world following the arrival of Christianity. As the process of conversion was done under the patronage of the colonizer, it is natural to presume that the process was detached from the value free neutrality.

This paper seeks to examine the impact on the indigenous peoples of the Manipur hills when their existing ways of thinking were encountered with the emergent ways of thinking brought about by Christianity. This paper further wishes to explore the contemporary social crisis of Manipur in the form of fragmentation and the rise of micro-nationalism as a consequent fall out of the concomitant divisive policy in their history, which engendered the denial of shared history.

The Impact of Christianity and the Culturocide

The British colonizers and missionaries when they came to Manipur also brought with them their cultural arrogance, as epitomized by the very phrase, "white man's burden". The day-to-day life of the indigenous people had an intimate and intricate relation with the nature and their natural environment. All the necessaries for their survival were derived from nature and its bounty resources, as economy was more or less sustenance based. It, thus, requires collective solidarity. Every production process like sowing and harvesting of food crops were carried out with the performance of community ceremonial rites. It can be cited by giving the example of the prevalence of winter festival: *Gaan Ngai.* among Kabui and Puimei, Gin Ngi for Liangmei and Hegangi for Jeme.[1] Similar such festivals with ritual performance called Kut were also in practice among the Chin-Kuki-Mizo people.[2] In their native religious practice appeasing the deity as a metaphor of forces of nature were carried out. But the westerners outrightly rejected such beliefs as useless superstition. According to noted historian G. Kamei, the Christian missionaries condemned the indigenous faith as animist and heathen, and they also tried to destroy the indigenous cultural and social practices. Robert K. Merton in his observation on the ceremonial rain dance of the Hopi Indians of New Mexico makes a distinction between manifest and latent function. The manifest function of it is their belief that the ceremony will bring rain they needed for their crops. The rain dance, Merton argues, also fulfil the latent function of promoting the cohesion of society.[3] Likewise the community participation in such ceremonial rites was functional for group cohesion. Thus a strong family and kinship ties and community networks were maintained through it. Their religion is thus, a reflection of society more specifically of collective representation.

But the missionaries, when they encountered these native social and cultural practices, they analyzed it subjectively with the values of their culture as the parameter to judge the worth of such native culture and practices. They, thus, count everything that is non-conforming to their culture as barbaric and uncivilized. It is evident from the writings of Reverend William Pettigrew who was credited for introducing Christianity in Manipur. Pettigrew in his observation on Tangkhul stated, "the people are very uncivilised. . . . They are demon worshippers and superstitious like the majority of the tribes around".[4] The patient endeavour of the Christian missionaries bore fruit, as they were successful in making the deeper penetrating inroads in the cultural sphere of the region. And the missionaries opposed many components of traditional culture even culture that "we might now think need not have been rejected as incompatible with Christianity".[5] What should be borne in mind is that this missionaries were working with strong support from the colonial authority. The attempt to address, why this colonialist was so intent to replace the local culture with the British culture will not be complete without studying the economics of conversion.

B.M. Bhatia while giving the reason for the creation of the middle class stated "by creating a social class in India with English test, English dress, English manners and lifestyle, a dimension which in turn would help the industrial revolution in England to keep up its pace".[6] The gospel of Christ thus obviously comes with the masked market driven interest of the colonizers. So, in the process, consumerism culture was promoted and this dismantled the base of their subsistence and self-sufficiency. Dr. K. Gailangam opines: "Much of the valued cultural life of the forefathers has been regarded as worthless, and as a result, our traditional socio-cultural life is slowly sinking as years past by".[7] Similar sentiments were also expressed by another Tangkhul scholar when he says, "The Christian way of life which in fact is the materialistic culture of the western colonizing nation, fine-tune our mindset and dull our native sense of dignity and identity consciousness that was local and indigenous was decimated and replaced by alien and foreign ways of livelihood".[8] Christianity also brought class-consciousness to the otherwise egalitarian tribal society as the gifted persons and the unclean ones are divided. So the new found 'holier than though attitude' makes the church member divided.[9] Christianity no doubt has been a great factor in the modernization of tribal society as it has been instrumental in abandoning the practice of head-hunting by the tribal, and also by unifying the tribes on the basis of commonality of languages by harmonizing the relations among them. In the process, they have also lost their connectivity with the past and their identity. It later became the mainspring for their denial of the shared history. Later development shows, the church from their earlier arrangement on geographical locations had to be reorganized and replaced by the language groups, namely the Liangmei, the Rongmei, the Zemei and the Puimei etcetra in the case of Zeliangrong, as the former has no longer become functional because of the growing tendency of emphasizing more on differences, heterogeneity and fragmentation. This trend has rather became a rule then an exception in the case of Hills people. The church, in such a situation were reduced to a centre for mobilizing intra-group activities which sometimes has advocated exclusionist tendency. It can be cited that the violent assault meted out to the residents of Khoibu Khangsim village at Tengnoupal sub-divison of Chandel district by the neighbouring Maring tribes and the destruction of their properties and houses on February 1, 2005 arises out of the formation of Khoibu Naga Baptist Association and opposition to it by the Marings. [10]

Imperial Manoeuvering and Ethnic Divide

The schism, developed and nurtured by the sectarian church, was further strengthened by exploiting the ethnic diversity during the Bristish colonial period as their policy towards Manipur. The need to classify and name the people with whom they came into contact and eventually governed was almost a compulsion with the British bureaucrat. The British rule encourage the tribal elites to form their tribal organisation. Mention can be made of Kabui Samiti (1934), Kabui Naga Association (1946), Zeilangrong Council (1947) the Kuki National Assembly (1946), Paite National Council, Gangte Tribal Union, Khunmi National Union (1947), etc. The tribes had asserted their ethnicity in social, economic, and political formation.[11] In order to have more bargaining power, there were ethnicisation of politics by the tribal elites.The problem of ethnicity thus arose due to absence of common political aspiration because of defective political socialization.That is why a pan-tribal identity that emerged with the categorization of all the tribals inhabiting in Manipur under two heads, Naga and Kuki by the British administrators for their convenience is still in conflicting hotch-potch identity. If, after Merger to India, the Manipur State Assembly which has representation from both the hill and the plain was not abolished it could have well served as the foundation of plural democracy under which roof, every brethren of Manipur can live in a state of harmony and peaceful co-existence. It should be remembered that, as a legacy inherited from the British, in 1951 after Manipur became a part of India, all the tribal groups were compelled to recognize themselves under the umbrella terms, namely "any Kuki tribe", "any Lushai tribe", "any Naga tribe", etc.[12] As they themselves are rooted out from history, the identity of the Nagas continue to have the characteristics of here to-day gone to-mmorow phenomena. It was best described by Sajal Nag by saying that the construction of the Naga identity went through perpetual shifts. Further he cited the example that in the 1940's, the Naga identity included even the Karbi and the Nepali but excluded all the Naga sub-tribes of Manipur.[13] The Naga Movement provided avenues for tribalism as there is a tendency to promote one's own tribe over the other tribes.[14] The cohesive solidarity with a mutually acceptable umbrella nomenclature is still eluding the Kuki-Chin group. All these had a bearing with the cultural blindness conditioned to them because of defective socialization through the inroads by the emergent ways of thinking brought by the Westerners. The Meiteis also went disarrayed with the conversion to Hinduism after embracing it by the Manipur king, Garibniwaj (1709-48. Because of it Bengali culture have overshadowed the Meitei identity. This has created an internal divide between the neo-convert and the non-convert including the Meitei who followed the indigenous faith and the hill tribes because of the practice of the notion of pollution and purity.The former branded the later as impure and polluted not only because of their being non-Hindus but also because of their drinking and non-vegetarian food habits which the neo-converts had abandoned after embracing the new faith. The Meiteis had afterwards succeeded in the process of de-Sanskritisation and what had emerged out of it was the synthesis, which was Sanamahi in ethos and Hinduism in outward appearance.[15] Thus by giving a repraisal to their past connectivity by indigenising Hindu religion and by reviving their native religion, Meiteis were able to reaffirm their affinities with the people in the hills of Manipur.

Development in the recent past has shown the darker side of ethnic identity assertion in the form of ethnic violence. In most cases studies on the ethnic clashes in Manipur has shown that demands for exclusive ethnic homeland were not compatible for harmonious co-existence in multi-ethnic situations. History doesn't only necessary mean the written records. In connection with this it will be worthwhile to cite from the response by the Red-Indian Chief, Seattle, in 1854 when he was asked to sell his people's land to the United States government: "Every part of this earth is sacred to my people every shining pine needle, every sandy-shore, every mist in the dark woods, every clearing and humming insect, is holy in the memory and experience of my people. The sap, which courses through the tree, carries the memories of the red man". Exploring the associated folklore, myths, and legends with the physical environment will surely reveal their close affinities and socio-cultural ties with each other among the peoples of Manipur which otherwise was buried due to the obsession for having an exclusive written record among various ethnos. In this way the people of Manipur can put back in the bottle, the genie that external forces had released to pursue the divide and rule policy.

NOTES

1. *Gaan Ngai,* Gaan Ngai Celebration Committee, Manipur. 2003.
2. *Souvenir.* Kut Festival, Imphal, 2002.
3. Merton, Robert K. *Social Theory and Social Structure*, Amerind Publishing Co. Pvt. Ltd., New Delhi, 1968.
4. Pettigrew, W., Ukhrul-1896, in *Souvenir,* Tangkhul Baptist Long Centenary, 1996.
5. Downs, F.S., *Essays on Christianity in North East India*, Indus Publications Co., New Delhi, 1994.
6. Bhatia, B.M., *India's Middle Class Role in Nation Building.* Konark Publihers Pvt. Ltd, New Delhi, 1994: 28.
7. Gailangam, K., Indeginisation of Christianity: Problems and Prospects, Proceedings of the Two Days State Level Seminar on *Tribal Identity and Development in Manipur,* 27th & 28th February, 2001, Imphal, organised by Manipur University Tribal Students Union (MUTSU).
8. Jajo, Y., Christianity and the Tangkhuls, in *Keluvim,* December 2004-February 2005, Vol.1, Tangkhul Baptist Church, Imphal.
9. Pamei, Dichamang., *Liberty to Captives*, A Zeilangrong Baptist Christian Church Publications, 1999.
10. Press release by Maring Uparup Assembly, *Poknafam* (Vernacular Manipuri Daily) February 6, 2005.
11. Kamei, Gangmumei, Ethnicity and Politics in Manipur, 8th Anniversary Special Supplement, Imphal Free Press, Imphal, 2004.
12. Nabakumar, W., Proceedings of the Seminar on *Ethnicity and Politics in Manipur,* Orgd. By National Research Centre (NRC) at Manipur University on 15th September 2003.
13. Nag, Sajal, 'North East: A Comparative Analysis of Naga, Meitei and Mizo Insurgencies'. In: Gill, K.P.S. and Sahni, Ajai (eds.), *Faultline,* Vol.14, July 2003.
14. Panmei Nehemiah, Naga Movement and its Ramifications, in *Nagas at Work*, Naga Students Union, Delhi (NSUD) Publications, Delhi, 1998: 97.
15. Kamei, Gangmumei, *Ethnicity and Social Change: An Anthology of Essays.* P.C. Jain Publications, Imphal, 2003: 46.

8

Globalisation, Monoculturalism and Ethnicity: A Regional Perspective

—P. MILAN KHANGAMCHA

It is now quite fashionable to say that, globalisation as an inevitable worldwide phenomenon has come to stay, and no country, society and individual can remain unaffected by it. The underlying superficial consciousness associated with keeping it as popular or fashionable utterance, prevents us from comprehending the seriousness of the complex issues of globalisation. Our discussion of this issue becomes more significant when it is considered that, monoculturalisation by information and communication technologies (ICT) enabled corporate globalisation is much more stronger than the capabilities of ethnic societies' to resist such an assimilative intrusion. Even to resist it, a society has to participate in it. This cannot be done without having ICT based infrastructures along with the conventional ones. Since, most of the societies are poor, backward and underdeveloped or simply lacks awareness or do not have the necessary leadership, these enabling infrastructure cannot be built. Hence, they cannot easily joint the processes of globalisation. Therefore, there is no question of their giving self-directed proactive resistance. Yet in some way or the other they may be swept by the global change. How to break this vicious circle is altogether a different question.

Whatever is the case, it is necessary to understand the problems of the multidimensional nature of the said global change and the inexplicable issues of identity inherent in the notion of ethnicity. What we mean by ethnicity is, ethnicity, which is not ethno-centric. To be realistic, the concept of identity associated with ethnicity would mean only those historically continuous, relatively stable ethno-cultural patterns identifiable during the respective stages of their assimilative growth and development. The continuity of those patterns as the constituents of an ethnic-identity depends upon the fact that, it is able to absorb incoming changes to its stride, rather than being swept away by them. But, under exceptionally abnormal circumstances, when it fails to withstand the onslaught of a much stronger mainstream cultural influence, it gets itself assimilated by the incoming influence. The socio-cultural, economic and political change heralded by the historically epoch making corporate globalisation is such an unprecedented international change which endangers the very survival of smaller and weaker traditional societies. Therefore, it is necessary to understand how globalisation induced changes are exceptionally strong enough to swallow smaller or even bigger traditional societies by it, ICT enabled homogenizing mono-cultural tendencies.

The survival question about an ethno-culturally pluralistic society of Manipur or any other North-Eastern states has become all the more serious because, it has been passing through certain unfavorable internal social conditions. But the enemy of an ethnic society as far as its survival question is concerned; it is, more within, then without. Such an internal enemy acts as a failed social immune system. Hence, the spreading of any mainstream culture as the external enemy to such a society becomes more easy in the absence of its' own social imbuement resistance. Hence, before we pass on to understanding the nature and functioning's of Globalisation as the external global causation which threatens the survival of an ethnic society, it is necessary that, we try to know the internal condition (which may facilitate the said external causation) first.

The magnitude of the society of the gravity of such an internal problems of Manipur Society is that, its ethnic identity, which had survived two great historical upheavals viz. The Seven Years' Devastation of Manipur by the much stronger Burmese army and the Anglo-Manipuri War (the Khongjom war) fought during 1891 at the Khongjom, an identity that had been painstakingly built up by successive kings, which is still continuing today, is now endangered ethnic specie. Though, as yet, it is not an entirely helpless situation, if the said undesirable internal social conditions continues, then, since, it acts as the absence of social immune system, our society is found to fall a prey to the assimilative power of globalisation. In the sphere of socio-cultural values alarming signs are beginning to manifest.

To state some of those signs, we may begin by saying that, during the last few decades of India's post-Independence era, Manipur Society has been passing though some mutually contradictory, polarizing and confusing phases of history. One such a situation, which in some way or other, today's people inherits, is the "intra-Meitei-community" contradictions involved in the attempts to have mutually antagonistic socio-cultural reconstructions as done by the upholders of sanskritisations and the revivalist trends initiated by Naoria Phulo. As the followers of these two schools co-exist in the same social space, till today, there are ongoing internal Social tensions and strafes, arising out of their mutual contradictions. In addition to this, there are various group based socio-political fragmentations and the increasing polarizations among them., and politics of ethnic confinement" and conflicts among an erstwhile mutually co-existing ethno-culturally diverse indigenous communities including the Meiteis.

With regard to the Meitei community, the relatively stable patterns of their ethnic identity are now beginning to crumble on the religious front. Perhaps, the prolonged rivalries between the Gaudiya Vaishnavas (followers of Manipuri Vaishnavism) and the followers of Sanamahi religion belonging to the revivalist tradition, has alienated many members of the same community and have started embracing other non-Hindu religious and sub-Hindu religions sects and movements. A large chunk of the community especially among the members of the generation belonging to both urban and rural areas has converted into Christianity. In addition to what has been stated, there may be other reasons behind such a religious cross-over . Though, very few, some took to a heterodox (nastic) religion system like Buddhism while some others has become the followers of Bahai cult. Among the sub-Hindu religions sects and movements, which have become popular among the followers of (Manipuri) Gaudiya Vaishnavism are:

1. The International Society for Krisna Consciousness (ISKCON),
2. The Divine Life Society, the Brahma Kumari Sect, who are mostly women,
3. The Satya Sai Baba cult etc. and
4. Sri Sri Ravi Shanker's Art of Living Cult, etc.

One significant thing about these four groups is that, while deviating to these intra-Hindu religious system, their followers have not given up practicing Manipur Vaishnavism. Different psycho-sociological interpretations may give for these religions adventures. One such possible explanation would be that, they are seeking some escape root from the unhappy social conditions. In the absence of a strong monarchical authority, the Meitei national trail of disunity and the free-mental outlook imbibed through modern education to which the Meiteis have a greater expose, and many other reasons, which are not possible to state here, might have caused them to seek such reformative path. Sociologically viewed, as such a social phenomenon , happening within few lakes of Meitei as the majority community of Manipur society, who occupies the same social space, are signs of social fragmentations, they act as stumbling block to effective social organisation and achieving the goal of social consciousness. The collective confusion caused by unchannelised social emerges make it difficult to stand as a united front which is a necessary social condition, needed for the sense of directedness towards solving various erases, which a society may come to face from time to time.

It is in the above, internal social condition of Manipur we are facing the shocking arrival of ICT enabled corporate globalisation. As discussed above, our society is not yet ready to face the challenges of globalisation. In such an internal social condition, it is no more a paranoid reaction to have the apprehension that, our ethnicity, folk based indigenous tradition, ethnic identity, lastly, and not the least, our value systems and rare virgin and diverse bio-resources are at stake. It seems that, the concerned government authority, members of the think tank of the public, members of the academia and relevant social groups are still in a semi-comatose state or their interest his elsewhere. It may not be too long before, with the arrival of the ill famous globalisation, its corporate Alibaba's cart away our idling and unexplored natural resources.

The nature of the complexity of the free-market economy of globalisation is such that, unless there are concerted multipronged efforts of all concerned in the society, we cannot successfully face its multifarious challenges. And, the required concerted efforts cannot come about, without group consciousness, that matured and enlightened social mind, the absence of which just referred to. Our position of strength as a pan Manipuri community would depend upon fulfilling this criterion of having self-conscious collectivity. Our enemy, within which we were talking about, is the absence of this social consciousness. Disunity as its' another expression is our internal enemy. Through this internal enemy we have been playing ourselves into the hands of the external enemy.

Because of the mutual-cohabitation by the communities of the ethno-culturally pluralistic pan North-East society, in a contagious socio-geographical space, no single indigenous society among them would be able to fight a lone war against the multipronged attack unleashed by the corporate mercenaries of globalisation. The only mantra for our survival today is that, we as distinguishable but inseparable societies of the Pan Manipur Society in particular and the greater North East Society in general stay connected to each other. This is not some intellectual utopia, but a logical corollary of our mutual co-existence in a common socio-geographical environment and also as members who share a long chequered and mutually interactive socio-cultural history. Our respective and relentless efforts for engendering socio cultural awakening have to be done with the ground reality of a pluralistic framework. We can be ethnic without being in ethno-centric confinement. Our return to folk studies had its parallel in the inception of the studies of folk traditions of European societies as a reaction to the social challenges caused by the Industrial Revolution. it is, in this context that, we are to discuss our legitimate apprehensions about the dangerous pitfalls of globalisation. Before we do so, we have to further elucidate the nature of our internal enemy with reference to the non-existence of self-knowledge.

A society's intimate knowledge of its own strengths, weaknesses and threat perceptions (SWAT) would not arise without "social-self-knowledge", self-esteem and self-confidence. Among all these, self-knowledge is the basis on which the other two stand. It is because of the lack of this social-self-knowledge that, we have been engaging among ourselves in the auto genocidal, internecine and mutually destructive intra-community and inter-community conflicts.

Our chronic anemia of group mind would mean that, our society is not still self-reflective enough to have a vital sense of directedness towards the attainment of the projected social goal. One cannot talk about any kind of social goal without its being directed by a group mind. And this social mind has to be located within the context of the dynamics of spatio-temporally continuous socio-cultural history. The meaningfulness of its continuation to the present should lie in its having a futuristic projection. And, on account of this, there cannot be the concept of a holistic social development as an ethno-culturally discontinuous, abrupt beginning. Again, we have to find our locatedness in the regional, national and international connectivity without which, by virtue of our being a member of the new emerging global valley, we cannot conceive army idea of wholesome social reconstruction. The new slogan: "Think global, act local" which is rightly termed as "globalisation" is a more satisfying version of the ethno-soul destroying, intrusive and unipolaristically overwhelming corporate driven concept of globalisation. Though, it would be difficult to implement whether we keep it as a mere wish or translate it into reality is in our hands. There has to be a satisfactory balance between tradition and change or between the ethno-autonomy and globalisation'. Those societies, which are unable to do, so are bound to parish.

With reference to the threat of the homogenizing and mono-cultural tendency of globalisation, we may mention the report that, nearly four hundred ethnic languages of the world have already become extinct and many more are on the verge of extinction, and thus are endangered. Mainstream languages replace the extinct languages. Such a phenomenon is only a symptom of a much more serious problem of a changed social-cultural patterns of a given ethnic community. There cannot be any discussion about a meaningful sense of ethnicity of communalities. Their problem lies in their inability to synthesize tradition and change. If the reality of socio-cultural variegatedness of the world has its charm and creative values, then such a lost is a lost for the rich and multifarious socio-cultural heritage of the world. This is the danger looming large to befall upon our relatively smaller and now weakened ethnicity, when it comes into conflict with the various impacts of globalisation.

Our traditional society is beginning to show some signs of loosing its long nurtured ethnic values. This goes with the changing behavioural patterns among the members of younger generation. They are wittingly or unwittingly leading a life on bought values which to some extent have, become discontinuous with their past. Most of them have become hooked to the ultra-modern value systems popularized by world wide advertisement and entertainment industries. They may be described as junk fast food loving and instant success driven MTV generation of the Coca-Cola variety. Their new found progressive and high-fi values, after having internalized exhorts them further to lead a life of sensuous indulgence in popular, vulgar, materialistic, hedonistic and morally outrageous liberal life style. Throughout the world this gnnxt is charged with leading a pleasure hopping, self-centered, mean and highly individualistic life style. They live in a world peopled with single hood (single status), live-in –partners, non-committal and one-night-stand relationships. In the matters of their sexual relationship they have a very casual and emotionally uninvolved approach. Now, this syndrome, which made an increasing inroad in metropolitan cities of India, so far, has not reached our society. But throughout the world it has become a dominant behavioural and value patterns among the members of the Gennxt. These cultural patterns are grafted in and through cable T.V., internet channels and mobile video phones with SMS capabilities, straightjacket to confused and defiled youths. With the breakdown of traditional methods of socialization, they live in a semi dehumanized and digitized virtual space. There is less human social contact. When the used and throw mentality which exist in the man-machine relationship, after having internalized in the highly atomized but, digitally connected individual psyche, is further externalized and extended to other fellow beings. The other always becomes a means to one's own ends someone to be disposed off or thrown away with after the casual purpose is served. This is a mentalistic turn entailed by the hyper-liberal values of the worldview of individualism (which is different from individuality). Now, this world view and its cultural patterns are on the verge of becoming global. The success of such an internationalized processes of cultural assimilation lies in the fact that it is based on an in-depth and carefully carried out market based research giving a sharp focus on the intimate details of those eternal and irreducible" human elements"(which exist on psychobiological and psycho-social planes) driving consumer behaviors. Thus, it is aimed at the exploitation and taping of those scrumptious and long repressed, lurking human psychological tendencies to sub-serve new liberal market interest.

It is quite possible that, the sensuously excited minds of adolescent people by M.TV etc based popular music and other forms digital entertainment programmes, found their necessary outlet in their now wide spread premarital sexual adventures in specially designed, semi dark corners of mushrooming local restaurants in the valley. We are too groups of the Manipur state. As yet, there is no awareness and concerted efforts among the intellectuals of our society as to find their social causations and also their legal, moral, socio-cultural and socio-pathological implications like their possible serving as one of the many causes for the alarmingly wide spread AIDS/HIV cases which has been gripping Manipur Society in particular and other North-Eastern Societies in general. Teenager sex and sexuality as such are normal facts of human life. In itself it is a moral. Thus, the issue of sexual –morality *vis-à-vis* our ethnic and conservative socio-cultural values should be discussed from an altogether different perspective which should be multi-prong approach in nature. Sexual urges like natural phenomena such as blowing of winds and flowing rivers are natural processes. As such, they cannot be repressed or stopped, but can only be diverted or canalized to a more socially fulfilling higher ends.

Therefore, we need to initiate public dialogue on the now non-existent introduction of sex-education, teaching life skills and social skills to growing up children to enable them to cope up by themselves with the problems of their own sex and sexuality, and also successfully face the rising complexities of life and society. We are yet to receive adequate attentions from the concerned government establishments and the members of the think tank of the society. Right now, they are in pathetic state collective vegetation.

If such a sexual behavioural problems of the teenagers are left in the hands of self-appointed morality police or cultural police men who carries out raids in all the targeted restaurants acquiring in the process the illfamous and notorious tag of local Talibans, through their aggressive, uncivil and undemocratic ways of dealing with such problems, then, the matter will aggravate even further. Of late, Manipur society is experiencing the social phenomenon of mob culture (mobocracy) who adherents go about demolishing homes and hearths of alleged criminals and immoral people of all sorts, giving untold inconveniences and dislocations from their homes to the innocent family members of those concerned socially undesirable elements. They get even ostracized outside their village or locality or even Manipur. No social scientists and other intellectuals and the academicians have come up with any plausible explanations for and solutions to those public issues. For the time being, what may be suggested here is that it is only the signs of all round system failure of Manipur society, where there is near total breakdown of governance. When rulers and administrator or non functional or their interest lies elsewhere, the power vacuum fill up by undesirable elements. Such a social condition is one of those features of our enemy within. It is quiet surprising that, in such a social situation, everybody seems be happy too happy and eager to join the bandwagon the elephantine India's 'Look East Policy', which just lunch symbolically through a trans-ASEAN car Rally as prelude to the impending imposition straight jacket grafting of globalisation to an unequal, confused, vegetating and digitally divided ethnic society of the North-East Region.

For a successful response to the problems and prospects of globalisation, not only for survival as an pan-ethnic community, but also for a holistic growth and development of society, it is necessary to understand what globalisation is. According to Alvin Toffler, it is an unprecedented, multidimensionally complex and ICT enabled worldwide change. It is also termed as Digital Revolution - the Revolution of the Third Wave. It is both qualitatively and quantitatively different from the preceding two global changes viz: 1. Agricultural Revolution, and 2. Industrial Revolution. It has heralded a new turning point in the human history.

Because of the application of Information Communication Technology (ICT which is the combination of computer and internet technologies etc.), with reference to its depth, endless scope and the blinding speed in which it occurs engendering every sphere of life and human activities, it acquires its distinctive and unprecedented character. It brings large-scale structural changes to our life, society, ways of thinking, attitudes, value systems, economic and political spheres. The free market economy or liberalisation brings major changes to the capitalist economy of the era of Industrial Revolution. Corporatisation and privatisation of government owned public enterprises and Institutions give a new dimension to the political structure of the globalised era.

Our conventional knowledge is not adequately equipped to respond to the problems of and prospects of globalisation. They need to be completely overhauled and recasted to meet its challenges. This results in the paradigm shift of knowledge and in the development of a new epistemic approach towards understanding its logic, driving forces and dynamics. The world wide network of digital connectivity with the criss-crossed speedy movements of knowledge on the Information Highways, make it necessary for everybody to be constantly on their toes and update their knowledge to catch up with its increasing frontiers. The knowledge workers of the Information Age must be ever ready to unlearn, learn and relearn. Otherwise, because of the speed and the ever-expanding scope of knowledge, and also due to the competitiveness of a highly liberalised and privatised capitalist economy, without the cutting edge knowledge, skill and understanding, surviving in an unpredictable and unchartered terrains of knowledge world is not easy. Hence, new vocabularies like knowledge worker, knowledge manager, knowledge industry or service industry, knowledge based society, information age and knowledge economy describe the paradigm shift in the globalised era knowledge situation. Such a new epistemic condition insists upon us to make ours as knowledge based society. Is our Manipur a knowledge based society even in the conventional sense, which has become more or less out of place with the changing world scenario of the nature and extent of digital connectivity. To stay connected to the worldwide electronic wave is the new mantra.

Manipur seems to be suffering from intellectual stagnation. It is perhaps, because of this that, we have not paid sufficient or no attention to the changes going on in our society as well as to the outside world. To do otherwise is, to fine their possible impacts on the society. The absence of such awareness is matched by our perverted enjoyment of an unhealthy sense of security in our respective, stagnating safety job cocoons. We may appear to be having an instinctive dread of treading the unknown and the unchartered domains of knowledge. We also may be having our animal instinct for protecting our respective knowledge territories. The interdisciplinary oriented researches are still discouraged and almost non-existent. We are not ready to compromise and make the necessary changes in the boundaries of our conventional knowledge for such a fusion research. Yet familiarity breeds contempt and we are bound to get perished due to our cognitive atrophy. The contradiction between tradition and change is thus, not confined only to the arena of ethno-cultural values. Because of our short sightedness and turning a blind eye to what is happening around us and the world, we are conveniently forgetting the scientific truth that, the capability for adaptation is the sign of a specie's being the fittest; and it is the only enabling law for its survival. Hence, for the purpose of protecting our ethnicity and also for all round development in today's globalised world, we have to have a holistic methodological approach to knowledge. Because, to enable us to cope up with the multidimensional issues of corporate globalisation, we need a different kind of knowledge which is different both in quality and quantity from our conventional ones.

The word survival associated with the mutual interractionism of ethnicity and mono-cultural tendencies of globalisation is not a simple concept. By survival, we do not mean that we remain barely alive. Survival is not the same thing with living. By simply talking about survival we are not talking about the later. Therefore, after having survived we have a long way to go till we reach the ennobled and dignified state of living. Before, we come to have the authentic life of living, we have to learn the art of "Surfing life" on the exploitative, inequitable and aggressive world wide waves of the Digital Revolution. Without survival, there is no question of living. Hence, the question as to how, our ethnic societies may survive and live in today's globalised economy still remains.

We have seen that, our various conventional knowledge are not equipped to provide any answer to the above question. As Alvin Toffler would say, only "Knowledge Economy" which is different from economy of knowledge can give the answer. Upto the pre-globalised era, international trade and commerce were functioning on the basis of the later which did not require any structural over hauling and recasting of traditional knowledge as per the logic and dynamics of globalisation. In such an epistemic situation the traditional boundaries of knowledge if not entirely disappeared, get shrunk. Interdisciplinary research does not mean they give up their fundamental researches which only the respective streams can do. Even, otherwise, our different apparently unconnected respective knowledge should reflect the veriegatedly interconnected world. The unity of existence, which saints and sages had intuitively experienced and had exhorted mankind to follow suit, as the precondition for peace, harmony and the welfare of the world, is now, in its own way affirmed by environmental science. The interconnectedness among the living and non-living things of the world which are only distinguishable but not separable is no more a myth or a convenient intellectual construct only as an environmental conservation strategy. Why people are making so much fuss about the nature of such interconnectedness? It may or may not be material; what does it matter? We only want "interconnectedness".

The concept of the unity of science and "conscillience" — "Unity of Knowledge" as coined by conservation biologist E.O. Wilson are welcome concepts of this new millennium of knowledge. It is, therefore, quite justified to say that, the syndrome of the airtight compartmentalisation of every academic discipline is symptomatic of the fragmented ego, which lives in a polarised world of disconnectedness. And, by doing this, all these while we have been missing the woods for the tree. By this, it is not mean that, we should neglect the tree for the sake of the woods. The notion of connectivity means making a proper balance between tree and woods. How can one miss the same truth of the proclamation of the ancient yore that, tiger protects forest and forest protects tiger; that, if we protect tree, then trees will protect us (vrikso raksati raksatah). In every sphere of life, the spirit of connectivity should be reflected. The survival of a tree to a large extent would depend upon the survival of the forest in which it grows and vice versa. But, it is also true that, we have been missing the woods for the tree for a long time. The enterdisciplinary studies are significant for solving social problems or any problem of existence. For, "knowledge sharing and collective learning would ensure human survival" (Leadership for the Unknowns, R. Gopalkrishna, *Business World*, 16, June, 2003, p. 48).

During the multidisciplinary dialogues on globatisation, the question of ethnicity constitutes one of the important perspectives. All the perspectives are inter-related to one another. Its importance lies in the fact that, if we are to speak from the context of structural analysis, though it is theoretically or in principle possible, there are practical difficulties in defending its cause. Because, ethnicity becomes embroiled in the intricate dynamics of corporate capitalism, privatisation, liberalisation, unipolarism, monoculturalism and consumerism etc. Identity as a necessary component of enthnicity, is no more a viable proposition in a world where the application of the digital technology makes every thing move very fast. No other cultural patterns, other than the ones created by the relevant corporate bodies can persist in such a hyper activated world. In such a situation our ethnic identity is forced to stand on the constantly shifting sands of time. Then, how can we talk about maintaining the stability of those weak and vulnerable ethnic value patterns as constituting our identity. In a fast forwarded life, people will hardly have time to look back to their past. The intense focus on the momentary present, even makes them unable to have a futuristic present.

The western value systems more precisely the American ones with tacit suggestion as more universal, attractive and plausible cultural patterns come in well packaged consumerised aesthetic forms. These are corporate created powerful cultural emageries with the suggestivity of neo-colonial contents. The empathising capabilities of consumerised aesthetic imageries have devastating communicable influence on those targeted neo-colonised ethnic consumers. This leads us to the under current of a consumeristic definition of man. The economic concepts of man as a consumer and society as consumer society are well matched with consumer products sold in abundance in the liberalised international market. The world is painfully unaware of the psychological, social, moral, economic, political and environmental fall out of such a consumeristic world-view. The Darwinian force which constitutively but surreptitiously operates within the dynamics of consumerism is dangerous for the marginalised, under privileged poor and weaker sections of the world. With the commodification of everything, even the die hard feminists are worried about the excessive marketisation of the feminine body through titillating corporate owned advertisement and entertainment consumer products. Is it the emancipation or a new bondage of women is a contentious issue. How true is said sex sales the most. Such a business thrives even better in sexually repressed traditional societies. The exploitation of such human weakness is a successful marketing strategy. It is no wonder that more than sixty percent of cyber business is based on all forms of pornographic industries launched online. It gives us the clues why sexually active teenagers and youths are getting hooked to the secret enclosures of cyber cafes. E-policemen and e-judicials are already grappled with cyber sexual crimes. Cyber child pornography is now a grave concern of all the right thinking people of the world. Even the ultra-liberal American society has no clues how to control such an unprecedented situation.

In order to stay connected to the world of consumerism, more and more young Indian women mainly college girls even those belonging to affluent families are regularly reported to be working extra-time or on part-time-basis in flesh trade. They cannot lead their hedonistic and consumeristic life style without having self earned purchasing power. Putting their bodies on sale in the business trip mixed with pleasure is the easiest means which is immediately available to young and vulnerable women. If it is at all bad or socially undesirable, no measures of external laws and morality policing will be successful unless they are made to see the undesirability of such an adventure. There has to be a changed world-view and attitude to ourselves and to the society at large.

The drive for fulfilling an unsustainable consumeristic life style is making young male members to resort to various crimes in the metropolitan cities of India. Now some psychiatrists have concluded that, obsessive urge to go on buying spree in multiplex malls which the consumeristic definition of man as a consumer entails or encourages, is a psycho-pathological condition. With consumerism in the hands of corporate giants, the dehumanisation, decay and degeneration of the present day human beings are almost near complete. The multidimensional natures of the concepts of equity, human rights, equality, justice and democracy etc. are the greatest casualties of the corporatisation and privatisation of the world. With the "trickle down effect" still non-existent in a highly unequal country like India, one may very well imagine the fate of those poor and rural people who constitute the majority of the country's total population, in the eventuality of the corporatisation of water. It is no more an unfounded fear. The human greed has already manifested in the increasing privatisation and industrialisation even of space.

The piece-meal and short sighted approach to developmental activities began since the inception of Industrial Revolution which was driven by a marriage of convenience between greedy capitalist and colonial powers perhaps, had started putting tremendous pressures on the scarce natural resources and delicately held equilibrium of ecosystem of the environment. The incestious rape of the mother Earth is still going on. Turning a blind eye to all the norms of environmental laws framed under the principle of Sustainable Development in the haste for constructing mega dams, which is still continuing today has resulted in large scale dislocation and displacement of indigenous tribal people from their natural habitations thereby denying them their rights to have access to their own natural resources for the sustenance of their life. Their folk life and its accompanying value systems, life style and their entire world view are intimately related to their natural habitations. This has become a serious concern for many well known environmentalists and green based N.G.O.s etc. Their united efforts were consistently ignored and stifled by the successive government authorities. The issues of environmental conservation, human rights violations, justice, democracy, equity and equality involved in the above problem are openly flauted. This is because, they are unable negotiate with the international funding agencies and capital market which force the Indian market to open up. Perhaps, having become blind by greed and to make political mileage out of these projects, it has not dawn to their minds how much and to what extent these developmental activities are putting the entire eco-system in irreversible environmental catastrophe. There is no free lunch. It comes with a price tag ; the rare and fast depleting natural resources must be privatised. And as a consequence, the poor people of the world will be left high and dry.

There are allegations that even government constituted environmental expert committee have been doctored to sex up the complex matters of environmental feasibility reports about various proposed corporate owned mega dams to be constructed in prime and virgin forest areas with rich bio-diversity. The existential woes of the people affected by Tehri Dam project has now reached epic proportions, the rest of the capitalist driven world is looking at the other way round.

Yet all hope is not lost, the multi-pronged global endeavours for environmental conservation led to the birth of a relatively new multidisciplinary science subject like environmental science. The world environmental concern had reached its climax with the signing of Kyoto Protocol. It has come into effect from the year 2005. Unfortunately, as an evil omen, the U.S. refused to sign it as it would halt its hidden agenda to be the neo-emperium. Many experts are now expressing serious doubts about the efficacy of such a protocol. Because, many of the signing member countries are continuing to contribute to global warming at an alarming rate. The refusal by the U.S. to ratify the said protocol is significant when we consider the fact that, as one of the most developed and industrialised countries of the world, it is the biggest polluter of global environment and contributor to global warming. The human capability to pollute the environment has even extended to the heavenly sphere of space. Even space has become partly privatised. Thus, we have come to hear about new vocabularies like space industry and space tourism.

The process of globalisation is not a spontaneous world wide happening. Then, what is its main driving force? That, it is an ICT enabled process of international change is quite another thing. It is also true that, the unprecedented ramifications which it effects cutting across every aspects of life is made possible only by the application of ICT. To quote one example, the psycho-cyber space has taken man to a new outological realm called virtual reality. Digital waves have given a new frontier of socialisation where through the mediation of such a wave human to human contact has become less emotional.

Yet, it is this wide electronic network which has tremendous potential of application which was unknown in human history, and it gives unimaginable powers and capabilities to those who wield it. It has wider implications of political economy of the world. And, moreover, it has direct bearing on our discussions about monoculturism of globalisation and ethnicity. Then, ICT as a technological tool may be either used or abused considering that, it is more abused than used, the question which may be asked is, who abuses globalisation. Since, we are living in a unipolar world, the U.S. is its main driving force. It uses digital revolution to sustain its neo-imperium status. This is the main reason why it refused to endorse the Kyoto Protocol.

To sustain this status, it needs endless supply of taped energy and bio-resources. With the hidden agenda to have a control over Iraq which is the second largest crude oil producing country of the world, under the pretext of safeguarding democracy, human rights, destroying axis of evil, WMD, peace, justice and liberty, it had invaded the helpless country twice. These secular ideals are untenable in a unipolar world. How can there be the spirit of tolerance and dialogue within such a world. During the run-up to the second Iraq War, its opponents were told: "you are either with us (the coalition of the willing) or against us." There is nothing in between "either" and "or". Symbolic logic would cold it the excluded middle" or exclusive disjunction. In the process, the U.S. had thrown the international democratic norms and the concept of sovereignty which were painstakingly built through centuries" toil into the winds. It had shocked and awed the world by the vulgar display of high tech weapons. The human history had not known a greater threat to global peace, order and stability, as it is now, under the presidentship of W. Bush I and II who is being referred to the most militaristically aggressive and interventionist of all U.S. Presidents.

Next to petrol as the source of energy (in addition to thermal and hydro-electricity) for driving the multifarious dynamics of the liberalised economy of world, is the fast depleting bio-resources. We have seen how in the scrambling for the control over petrol, what the U.S. could do to Iraq. In an unequal, digitally divided world where even the relevant conventional infrastructures are non existent the hunt for bio-resources by corporate giants directly affects the social, economic, cultural and political interest of ethnic communities of the world. Ignorance of this fact, may turn out to be very costly for a bio-resource rich region like the North-East India in the future. The ideas of bio-piracy and gene hunters are not some non-existent ghosts imagined by idle minds. Many countries are already having stringent environmental laws to protect their bio-resources. In today's patent raj, enough social and legal measures are required to conserve and protect our various forms of indigenous knowledge. The corporatisation of our unexplored rich varieties of flora and fauna, via legal or illegal methods would tantamount to making our successive future generations, captive markets for rich countries. Nothing can be done to prevent these, unless, there is public awareness and a strong political will.

The symbiotic existence between ethnic people and their natural surroundings are reflected in their folklores, folk medicines, folk arts and literatures etc. Their access to their natural environment provides them with their means of sustenance. Thus their social, economic and cultural life are inseparably related to their mutual co-existence with surrounding forests, hills, meadows, plains, lakes, wet lands and rivers. We now hear books on environmental themes entitled Ethno-Botany and Ethno-Zoology etc., only those who are unaware of the concept of "knowledge economy" as the new epistemic reality of the globalised world would scoff at it. Such books with a new thematic turn reflecting a new "knowledge condition" has its value for environmental conservation. Any science which has no human touch would be dangerous for mankind. We had only seen that happened after the completion of the Manhatten project. The world has changed a lot since. It is quite probable that Japan was shocked and awed to keep the whole world in the defensibly by creating fear psychosis. Of course, the question still remains "if" Japan was not atom bombed, what would have been the fate of the world today?

Hence, having an in-depth study of folk traditions, not only has relevance to our concern about ethnic identity, but also possessing proper knowledge of the symbiotic relation between folk societies and their natural environment is one way in which we may become aware that severing such a link would do irreparable violence to both human and nature. Such a violence may lead to far reaching consequences even of the world. This is one of the truths which under lies sustainability of development.

Since, bio-technological industries will be the main business of this millennium of knowledge, and it is one of the special features of digital revolution, countries or regions having virgin and rich bio-resources are considered to be living with gold mines. But, because of human greed, now, the world has been left with only few countries having unexplored vast virgin forest areas with variegated species of flora and fauna. Since, pharmaceutical and agro-based industries would depend upon the availability of bio-resources, and their need in life is quite obvious, they have a significant place in this globalised world.

The increasing attentions received by the North-Eastern states, from many foreign dignitaries of the developed countries who are major players of the globalised economy of today, and even India's LEP are to a greater extent based on keeping in view of the above facts. Because, the North-East region has been identified as one of those very few countries having virgin and rich bio-diversity. Therefore, the strong currents of the dynamics of global political economy, which on the cultural level has already infiltrated into our society should not make us drawn by it. There is no justifiable reasons for us to consider the said attention we are beginning to receive as the divine grace of the "White Man's Burden".

If the new-imperium (U.S.) under the megalomaniach presidentship of W. Bush I could do, what it had done to Iraq, just for the sake of the black gold, and the violent conflicts are still going on with renewed vigour under W. Bush II, then, there is no reason why we should not suspect the said undue attentions.

Globalisation means no country for too long can remain with its market closed to the outside world. Countries will be forced to open their market to the business houses of the world. So, we cannot forever remain with our gates closed affixed on it with the sign "No Corporate through fare" or not for sale to MNCs". What the Loktak Project had done to the lake's ecosystems and the socio-economic sustenance of the local population inhabiting at its adjoining areas are now well known. The proposed Tipai Mukh Dam is still embroiled in controversies. Apart from few claims and counter claims between the government authority and the opponents of the project, the matter has not, as yet become a public issue. Going by the track record of the state and the successive central governments, mostly in such matter, it is the government which ultimately triumphs.

The futility of such dams or any other developmental activities undertaken by the government is that, the economic gains accrued to the national income do not reach the majority poor of the country. The high alarming rate of suicide, by the frustrated farmers of India is being reported very often by the newspapers. As far as the absence of the "trickle down effect" is concerned, since the NDA government's much hyped and sensationalised claim of the "India Shining" has now turned out to be a myth, through such devastating privatisation based developmental activities, the poor, the marginalised, under privileged, rural and indigenous people will always stand to loose.

With the reports of the centres flawed draft forest and environmental policy of the North-east region coming in, and, since such a defective policy, which is wanting in many respect with major loop holes, is only a prelude to the country's LEP, the ethnic tribal people of the region are, perhaps awaiting a major irreparable lost. How are we to ensure the sustainability of the possible bio-resources based, globalised era developmental activities? India's undemocratic ways of dealing with various public issues and its capability to bulldoze any valid public opinion do not instill in us with any hope for finding suitable answers to this question. That, it has not yet become a public issue would mean that, the society has no awareness that, there is such a problem awaiting to befall upon an unsuspecting mass. Ultimately it boils down to the non-existence of collective consciousness in our fragmented and multi-dimensionally polarised society. There is no self-contradiction in saying that, a society exists, and at the same time, it has no social consciousness. It is that individually locatable consciousness which is social; the same experience which exists in the inter-subjectively of every similar minded members or the shared common experience. That is, what is lacking among merely congregating unconnected individuals.

The people of the North-East India are like the seven sisters, who even while sitting pretty well on a vast gold mine of natural resources, because of ignorance of such a fact, they are so poor that, very frequently, they have to go with their begging bowls to Delhi for alms. There cannot be a greater bondage than this. It is the bondage of their own ignorance - the internal bondage exploited by the vested interest. Unco-ordinated, disorganised and unchannelised, mutually polarising groupism based socio-political activism, are self-serving activism, sans collective consciousness. That is, there is no inter-subjectivity or share common experience.

Therefore, before the centre's LEP is materialised at least for the sake of participatory democracy and decentralisation, the region disparately needs a local Alibaba having deep self-awareness, who only could open the said treasure house, and put the region on the global treasure map of free-market economy from a position of strength. But, there is a long way to go. Because, India is yet to be fully democratic and implement the decentralisation process as necessary socio-political felicitation of its kind of plurality. Without them, the country's LEP would be unbeneficial or unequitable to the local indigenous people. The North-East region in general and Manipur in particular have to find their respective slots in India's scheme of things under its LEP. Otherwise, we will be more silent spectators to the endless business transactions to be happening with or without our own natural resources, under our own noses. While these are mostly from the contexts of bio-technological and environmental issues, on the socio-cultural level, the impact of globalisation has been already observable in the changing value systems of our youths. This will be further compounded after the full implementation of the above policy. Not only on the cultural domain, because of the railway line and trans-national highways to be built and likely migrant flows towards the state, the demographic composition of the state may become drastically changed overwhelming the indigenous inhabitants. Large inflow of Hindi speaking and Bangladeshi migrants have occurred during the last decade in the Imphal city and adjoining areas. This likely demographic movement, if not checked, as it is already happening, the migrants may completely outnumber the local population. As it has been stated before, even in this case, like it is in Assam, it is yet to receive public's attention. By the time people becomes fully aware, it may turn out to be too late. We already had an unsuccessful violent student's movement against foreigners during the 1980s which was brutally suppressed by the security forces.

Returning to the socio-cultural issue as having a direct bearing on ethnicity, when greater and greater numbers of younger people the world over are getting addicted to the ultra-liberal American cultural patterns, can our own youths be left far behind. The gennext or the MTV generation - the "I am me" type has to some extent started arriving at our traditional social scenario. The American culture which has become homogenised as western culture is not the same with European culture. But, even the European societies having their own age old values are now unable to resist the American cultural invasion. At the same time, though it is insignificant we do hear the interesting report of another equally popular American youth cultural icon, Avril Lavagner of the rock and roll group, being from conservative family background is not so revealing or body displaying like Britney Spears. This is a bit of an information of America's own version of the conflict between tradition and change. She even openly critices Britney for her morally outrageous ways. It is quite heartening to hear. Yet, in the globalised era unipolar world, the American or the western socio-cultural values are spreading like wild forest fire.

What are the possible reasons for the instant success of such a value system having homogenising mono-cultural potentialities ? It has become a lethal cultural weapon in the hands of corporate marketing Dronacharyas. Its success correspondingly means, the failure of the traditional societies to resist this world wide phenomenon.

The success of such a cultural invasion may be due the capability to cleverly synthesise certain aspects of the individual psychology and social psychology, a well researched aggressive marketing strategy, and a global corporate controlled print and electronic media which, directly or indirectly functions to subserve the unipolar interests of the U.S. This had become evident during the Iraq War II, when the neo-conservatist think tank of the white house whose members are themselves major shareholders of multinational compaines, had summerily dismissed any suggestion about multipolarism, in favour of unipolarism. The American Global linterest pushed through its foreign policies, under W.Bush has become more militaristic in imposing its "American Justice" on whichever is the helpless country it chooses to. Its rhetorics of a new world order, justice, liberty, world peace and lastly democracy etc. are being projected as the justification for its assumming the self-styled global moral authority and the role of international policeman. This big brotherly mind set of the Uncle Sam persona of the Paxamericana leads to the outright rejection of any proposal for multipolarism and multilateralism. This is not simply an unfounded theory but something which has become a reality. There is nothing which the world community can do about it. This has serious global political implications. If unipolarism is the ground reality, it cannot be co-terminus with the above secular ideals which the U.S. projects as its saving agenda.

The above analysis is crucial for our understanding of the world wide popularity of the American value systems and life style etc. among the youths. Such an analysis is necessary for finding a solution to the survival issue of ethnic societies. There are certain psychological reason for the rejection by the members of ethnic societies of their centuries old traditional values. Such a denial follows the inability of those traditional values to have a lasting hold on the collective psyche. Since the collective cannot remain vacuous for too long, it seeks a more promising, satisfying and attractive cultural values mainly belonging to the mainstream society. They find these new values as a refreshingly liberating force enabling them to break free from the monotonous and repressive traditional values which are being perceived by them as out dated. These de novo values are considered as fashionable by them and therefore, it is quite natural that, those new liberal values become their life style statements. In their changed persona, they also wear a changed attitude in their own notion of self-identity.

If any concession is to be given to the desirability of effecting a synthesis of tradition and change of which history had not known a smooth transition, it is because, on the basis of socio-biological truth, it would ensure the survival of any ethnic society. Adaptation is the strategy of evolutionary biology programmed in the species for enabling the survival of the fittest. And the fittest are those who can successfully adapt to the changing social environment which are beyond their control. As this would be a continuous process, our ethnic identity goes on redefining itself in its spatio-temporal continuum. We speak of identity only in respect of those relatively stable cultural patterns. But the matter of traditional identity, somewhat becomes complex when we discuss about it in the context of post-colonial history. While we are yet to come out of the residual colonial hangover, it seems that, we are once again ushered into another but a new colonial era. The people of former colonies of the world like India, still perceives the more advanced and modernised societies of their former colonial rulers, as having superior value systems, and as such, they are considered as universal role modals to be emulated by the rest of the (third) world or former colonies. This may be more unconscious than conscious. This presents us with the psychological factors relating to identity. Most probably, it is to instill this perception as a living cultural residue, in a subtle manner, that commonwealth association exists. As stated earlier, this cannot happen, unless those recipient societies view their traditional identity and value systems associated with it as inferior, outdated and not progressive enough to be relevant with the changing times. Now cultural anthropolists are of the contention that, there cannot be inferior or superior cultures. Expression like savage and primitive etc. as being referred to indigenous tribal and abo-original people by colonial thinkers are now, therefore, taken as biased statements.

Apart from the said colonial hangover, another possible reason why western value systems, their beliefs tastes, sensibilities, ways of thinking, attitudes and life style are believed to be the superior role modals by most of the former natives and a perception handed down to their descendents would be that, those superior societies also possess the cutting edge and state of the art know how in the fields of science and technology, advanced and affluent economic status, enabling and favourable social conditions.

When, we are heralded into the post-liberalised era, the above image of the western societies and their value systems are even more strengthened. This is made possible by the increasing digital connectivity of the world and the corresponding shrink of the psychological space among people belonging to different geographical isolated countries, and the increasing movements of knowledge workers from one country to another country which are now existing as members of the emerging Global Society. Due to the cross-cultural dynamics of such human movements, changes in the traditional socio-cultural values of them is quite natural. But, it is more of assimilative transition of traditional value systems to dominant mainstream cultural systems and not the other way round. We hardly see American and other western or European people wearing Indian dresses or following any other socio-cultural values of the country. There is no other explanation behind the collective fixation and frenzy for cricket by the people of former colonies. By the same logic, we do not find Americans, Chinese and Japanese or any other societies, having a more ancient civilizational history and strong national identity showing any sign of interest in such a commonwealth game as cricket. How can one fail to see the point ? The people of Bengal are now having a cross over from their collective hysteria for football to cricket, because like many great luminaries of their community Saurav Ganguly has also placed their national image on the international arena.

In this information age, those alien cultural patterns are available in neatly packaged aesthetico-commercial forms, as cultural products right in our living rooms, in those intimate cyber space provided by the internet, and even while walking down the street in our mobile video phones. We in our kind of society have no capability or no interest to deconstruct and uncover those multilayered commercially packaged cultural imageries, and expose their hidden truth. The art of packaging has now achieved the status of a global industry. It is not difficult to see what would be the likely consequences of such a scenario.

Such packaging industries can make or unmake cultural patterns, and transmit them at ease to the entire world, in the above manner. The inherently redeeming qualities of those ultra-liberal, individualistic and progressive values popularised via the medium of ICT seem to authenticate those youth-oriented Americal cultural values as global role modal. Britney Spears is right now the reigning queen of the global youth role models whose fashion signature carries multimillion dollar values and as such, she could at ease push through instant world wide sale of teenage based textile products. She and many super models are capable of making world wide hysteria of fashion waves. The gregarious human nature, gullibility, the herd instinct, low self-esteem, lack of self knowledge and confidence, and the law of conformity make the task more easy for the global fashion industry. These corporate sponsored icons can simultaneously destroy other tradition found values, and create a homogenised and neatly packaged assembly line cultural values.

The said liberal values are spread throughout the world with the strong undercurrent of psycho-normative insistence, These neo-cultural patterns are propagated with missionary zeal not for their own sake, but only as a cultural ploy for creating favourable psycho-social environment of captive consumers on whose taste, belief systems, sensibilities, attitudes and the over all world views, the acceptability of the cultural products of multinational companies would depend. No consumeristic world view (consumerism) could ever thribe without first creating a prior taste for those consumer products.

But, there can be also mutual influence between consumer behaviour and consumer products. Because, for those recalcitrant-orthodox members of larger and well established traditional societies, the products have to be specially customised to suit their cultural tastes. With this intention, Japanese textile companies are manufacturing different ethnic based Indian saries like Gujarati sari etc. and Chinese manufacturers are flooding Indian local markets, with cheaper and qualitatively better religious-cultural products like fire crackers and *puja* items which Hindus widely use during Diwali (multi-level marketing). But such traditional societies with well trenched value systems are beginning to shows signs of crack. Through corporate funded well intentioned studies of consumer behaviour, business houses are able to manufacture, nurture and instill newer artificial wants and needs through the ubiquitous ad and entertainment industries and produce consumer goods accordingly.

The globally popular beauty pageants, endless fashion shows and cat walks by scantily clad young models on the one hand, and parallel mushrooming of cosmetic products, fashion technology schools, beauty parlours are not mere coincedents. The concept of beauty which used to be ethnic-cultural specific is not more in vogue. The notion of beauty at least on the physical plane has become globalised by maintaining a standardised bodice. This goes with the scrambling for cosmetic surgeries mostly among young women to match with the corporate designed semi-manufactured concept of beauty. As far as such a universalised idea of beauty is concerned, Wittgenstein's view that a science of aesthetics is impossible is being challenged. Beauty no more lies in the eyes of the beholder. It has been raised by hook or by crook to a level of objectivity by setting a standard of beauty. It is these assembly line models who are used as bait for catching customers.

The said standardisation of beauty is not merely done on the physical plane. The concept of beauty with brain is speaking of it in the holistic sense. The notion of integrated personality with reference to its various identifiable parameters like the levels of I.Q. aptitudes reasoning ability, group discussion, and various other tests are used for testing their intelligence. Hence, such a concept of beauty attemps to purge those traditional features of it which places women to an inferior position to man. It is a notion of the era of girl power, women's empowerment and gender equation etc. The semi nude condition through which super models and reigning queens of beauty such as Miss World and Miss Universe are visually presented though have their commercialised titilating value, nevertheles, is sign of her new found self-confidence. Whether it is a picture of an emancipated woman or a marketing ploy or lastly a women first of all as an individual has the right to display her body for name and fame or personal excellence are still to be answered.

One psychological fall out of such a concept of beauty is that, many young women all over the world who somehow failed to reach its standard specially on the physical level like the twiggy or the ultrathin image is making young girls to go on the fasting spree and are mostly showing the symptoms of anoraxia. Those who cannot just shed their extra fats or do not have the expected height are already suffering from inferiority complex and found themselves having appointments with psychiatrists. But the beauty industry thribes on. Unless a product is standardized, it will not have commercial value. In spite of the cognitive ability test involved in the two world level beauty contests, the commodification and the corporatisation of feminine body are quite obvious. With such a homogenised concept of beauty which is making global waves, it is quite puzzling to understand how the Johnsberg Declaration had stood for the need of conserving human diversity.

That, the conservation of human diversity has close relationship with environmental conservation has already been discussed by showing their underlying social, economic, cultural psychological, political issues and ethnicity. No consistent preservation of human diversity may be had if the mono cultural tendency of globalisation becomes a world wide trend. Because, Manipur as an ancient civilisation and as having an historically continuous ethno-culturally pluralistic society, is already affected by the cultural values of the mainstream India and the West. Among most of the indigenous tribal communities of the North-east India, excepting dress, food and language etc. after their conversion into christianity which took place during the colonial era and after, almost all of them had discontinued with their folk cultural traditions like their belief systems, customary rites and rituals and music, specially the use of indigenous musical instruments. Some of the Kabuis of Manipur somehow did not come under the Christian influence. Hence, they are still practising various aspects of their folk tradition. Yet, some forms of socio-political awakening seem to be making various ethnic tribal people like Kuki, Kabui and others to celebrate their respective annual festivals, with funfair.

The only way to resist the ongoing cultural homogenisation by the processes of globalisation is spreading public awareness about the importance of preserving and popularising various folk cultural tradition like music etc., specially among the youths. A change of attitude in the way in which, we look at our folk tradition requires. Though, it is not easy to judge what is to be conserved, there may be ways to do the task.

If the youths of the state are not having any taste in their own folk music etc., it is the responsible members of the society to be blammed. Culture as acquired collective habits may adapt itself to the emerging social conditions and changing tastes in people. But then, taste itself, though is quite natural, while keeping in view of democratic norms, it may be necessary to have some form of social control as per its desirability or undesirability. It may not be an easy task, yet, it is to do with making a proper balance between individual and collectivity. When there are all-round social confusions, system failure and the associated sense of cultural vacuum, it is reflected in the individual. This is what is being proposed here as the unconscious or semiconscious syndrome which our youths suffer. Such cultural vacuum in them is matched by their mass hysteria and engrossment in popular art forms like music and cinema. Except some very few, most of the so-called Manipuri popular musics and popular cinemas which are churned out in plenty because of the use of digital movie cameras, leaving video movies ways far behind, not only are of poor aesthetic taste both in contents and forms, but also do not portray any ethnic character which would justify the title Manipuri attached to them. Fortunately many right thinking members and social groups are now beginning to become at least aware the gravity of the problem which is more or less of serious concern in respect of our ethnicity. We all know that many of our folk art forms like Pena, Khutlang Ishei and Khongjom Praba are endangered, Khubak Ishei is already extinct through socio-cultural atrophy. Who has to be blamed for this? This became evident when, even after wide spread notifications, only one female student had turned upto participate in the competition section of the M.U. & MACS co-sponsored Two Day Folk Music Festival for an AIDS/HIV Free Manipur held at the G.P. Women's College, during November 28-29, 2003. One more section under the competition section which could not attract any participant was on the topic of a still misunderstood sex education. It is no wonder that, the said popular art forms are to a greater extent lacking those necessary ethnic traits which would support their carrying the tag 'Manipuri'. Many of them are straight jacket imitations (it is no wonder that Plato calls art as mimesis) of the "formula music" and "formula movies" of the confused Bollywood's entertainment industry. In this manner, such popular aesthetic taste would be further perpetuated down to the next generation and so on. Such a decline in the level of taste and artistic sensibilities would reveal the shallowness of the collective consciousness — that lack of depth of experience, the immaturity, ignorance, decay and degeneration of "the life of minds" (B. Russel). This again is only one of those signs of identity crises of the collectivity of the Manipur society which has been trapped in a transitional and confusing social condition multidimensionally criss-crossed with puzzling issues engendered by the forces of tradition and change. Unlike other major changes which had occurred in human history, the application of digital technology only deepens the seriousness of the issue under discussion.

In such a directionless social condition, an entire younger generation in different formative stages of their growing up personality are left unattended by their busy parents to be baby sitted by cable T.V.s, and many adolescents are already seeking socialisation in those secret enclosures of mushrooming cyber cafes where they surf though the waves of cyber hedonism or e-hedonism. This is made possibly by digital revolution. Socialisation processes has metamorphosed from the semi-urban condition of the valley to the e-based virtual social space. But the case of Manipur society is quite peculiar. Because, ours is not yet a fully urbanised society like other metropolitan cities of India or the rest of the world. The so-called Imphal city is still almost like or even below the suburbs of these megacities and towns of the rest of the country. In many respects the valley society is still having its rural character. In this condition, its youths are ushered into the hi-fi cyber-society. The emotional needs and energies peculiar to tender and vulnerable sexually active and digitally activated teenagers are not properly managed, organised, and channelised towards the attainment of social goals. What the government level think tank (if there is one), intellectuals, experts, parents and teachers have not been doing is quite naturally taken over by corporate commissioned "knowledge researchers" on consumer behaviour. The raw and natural sexual energies of growing up children are taped, exploited and commodified. It is quite natural that, an over-exposed and over-excited psycho-sexual drives are saught to be satiated. Since, the society is still tradition bound, the pent up sexual urges of the youths have no outlet. This has direct correlation with the rise in the numbers of small roadside restaurants whose owners are quick to case on this fact. Based on the economic principle of demand and supply, they are only providing the covered up facilitations needed for fulfilling the sexual gratification of the teenage youths. Inspite of morality policing the business is thribing surreptiously. The society seem to have no awareness of the legal and moral implications of such an emerging social phenomena. It is the commercialisation of a very normal process like sexual urges of teenagers in the semi redline corners of the said restaurants who seem to be running unorganised sector of small scale sexual industries. During the last few years there have been newspaper reports of various social groups assuming pro-active roles to check such illegal sexual trade. Of course, the youths themselves are not to be confused with sex workers. The question is only about those who make encashment out of the teenagers' sexual adventures. Since, the matter is very complex, thorough brain storming dialogues are required for seeking solution for such a problem. It is not sure, how, such a psycho-social phenomenon because of their inevitability, long left alone by more scientifically oriented and enlightened advanced societies of the west may be tackled by such a confused society. The process has not begun yet. But, good or bad, the local upholders of traditional values, like the Siva Sainiks in other states and their similar hords, have already taken the pro-active social responsibility to close down the said restaurants which come into frequent skirmishes with them. How far, it would be successful and what may be the likely social implications of such a conflict between tradition and change are only well known to the social scientists. In the process the youths are the first casualty.

It may not be an unwarranted thing to say that till the social scientists are awakened by some divine intervention from their vegitating slumber and become illumined by the emergent social consciousness, what are being stated thereto are mere wishes. In the meanwhile in their confused and unguided life, teenagers are herded into restaurants where the possible danger of their being infected by AIDS/HIV virus is very high. Though, still it is an unchartered and explored domain, and to that extent, what is to be viewed here may be by way of offering suggestions, even the case of the wide-spread socio-pathological syndrome of drug abuse and various behavioural problems of the society's youths, may be the symptomatic of a confused society passing through its transitional phase. Whether, the transition to some future social condition would turn out to be desirable or undesirable, only time will tell, but the history of social evolution does not bear witness to the fact that, any social change is purely mechanical or natural enough to justify those who are awaiting for the socio-natural process to take its own course. Finding social causations and making of necessary and possible predictions so as to achieve the goal of social engineering are still needed. Yet, any such vital enterprise has to be done, not as an abrupt upstart but keeping in view of the spatio-temporal continuum of the society which encompasses its past, present and future. This is not possible without the deepening of social consciousness.

The continuing youth's unrest for the last three or four decades, the fregmentedness and polarisation among various organisations and the mind boggling numbers of social groups which according a report has already run upto nearly four thousand or so, cutting across caste, creed, religion, communities, political groups and gender, that too in such a socio-geographically small society, may not be a healthy sign. In such a state of disunity, the said fregmentedness, directionlessness and their underlying absence of social consciousness, talking about identity, relative or otherwise may not be easy, if not impossible. The youths are only victims of such a socio-pathological condition. Just merely passing it off only as a mere transitional social phase would be too convenient an explanation.

As stated earlier, in this globalised era, it is dangerous not to be self-determined. This cannot come about without collective self-knowledge, the creatively growing and dynamic ethnic self embodied both in content and form in those relatively stable socio-cultural patterns in their spatio-temporal settings. Perhaps this is what is missing in the state's pluralistic collectivity. It is this future which is now under threat and its present is already showing the signs of the implending danger. These threats come from commercially designed corporate owned alien cultural products (which youths are not ready to admit as alien or undesirable) which are packaged to rouse empathy from impressionable youths all over the world. Since, these are carefully packased by integrating in them certain irreducible and universal psycho-biological traits of human nature as they are discernible in their social embodiments, they are easily assimilated by consumerised youths, especially by those who have been living with those lurking, haunting and repressed urges.

In this context we may dwell on some aesthetic aspects of ICT based advertisement and entertainment industries, and their use of aesthtic techniques with devastating impact on the youth consumers. Who constitute more than sixty percent of the global population and a similar percentage of e-businesses is pornographic business. The debates about the borderline case of pornography versus erotics are still going on. In this context we do share with the concerns of Plato and Marx and many others with regard to the need for making a proper balance between art and the requirements of life and society. It may have to be done without making art to surrender its autonomy. The theoretical issues involved may be kept aside for the time being. But in this age of digital revolution with the emergence of virtual reality in the cyber space, the dirty commercial objectives based on over-exciting human tendencies, have used the powerful potential of artistic communication for making the "suspension of disbelief" in the minds of an already prepared consumers.

Nowadays, intellectuals are beginning to realise the merits of art forms mainly music and drama, as the later Plato did, as having therapeutic and pedagogic values. Art instills values without teaching. Because of art's cathartic potential, it is a good means for the channelisation, enculturing and nurturing of taste and refined sensibilities in the minds of the growing up children. Therefore, the role which art assumes in shaping personalities of young people cannot be overlooked and should be in safe hands. The application of ICT to music and histrionic techniques for commercial purpose is one of the easy ways in which the unipolar objectives of globalisation is imposed upon a helpless world.

9

Globalisation and Cultural Interactions in Manipur

—JAGAT THOUDAM

Introduction

In this paper a brief attempt will be made to analyse critically the impact of Cultural Globalisation in Manipur society. Although it is located far from the metropolitan and urban industrial complexes of India, Globalisation is not far from this landlocked hilly state. The changes brought by the development and progress of technology, transport and revolution in communication and information technology have globalized every events and happenings across space and time. This globalizing tendencies and phenomena distinguish modern society from primitive and traditional society both quantitatively and qualitatively. Process of globalisation of institutions and ideas occur at multiple levels as a result of various socio-cultural and politico-economic consequences which are unfolding before us. And our society is also not immune from the consequences.

The topic of globalisation and cultural interactions in Manipur includes three vital elements, viz. "globalisation", "culture" and the unfolding process of Globalisation interacting with the cultural elements of the Manipur Society. Is it appropriate to call it cultural interactions in our social context or simply a superimposition of ideas and cultural patterns upon the relatively poor, backward economy and smaller political and cultural community like our own? Can the smaller cultural groups ever resist the multifarious onslaught of Western Cultural hegemony?

Genesis/Meaning

To be more precise and focus to the topic, it is pertinent to understand the meaning, nature and extent of the term globalisation. Even though there cannot be a single definition of Globalisation, the generally agreed meaning of the term is the process of shrinking the world in space and time, constant inter-connectedness and more trade across the world. Looking from this perspective, the genesis of Globalisation can be traced back to the beginning of the Industrial Revolution which occurred during the hundred years after 1780, which witnessed the first break through from a rural, handicraft economy to the invention of new technology for enhanced productivity- to be dominated by the urban, machine driven manufacturing and search for the Colonies to provide market goods and raw materials.

However contemporary meaning and nature of globalisation is radically different from the earlier one. Today, due to the revolution in information, communications and transport technologies, changes in the power balance because of World War I and II and institutionalization of globalisation through Bretton Woods's institutions (IMF & WB) and subsequently WTO. It goes without saying that all these institutions are dominated by a few big powers particularly the USA. Today globalisation is associated with constant liberalization and privatization, reduction of trade barriers and tariffs and free flow of capital and commodities from one part to other part of the globe and drastic reduction in the regulatory role of the State.

The concept of free market economy and *laissez-faire* policy propounded by such classical liberal thinkers viz. Locke (1632-1704), Adam Smith (1723-90), Jeremy Bentham (1748-1832) and Ricardo were institutionalized by the Bretton Woods (1944), which regulate the global trade for about 25 years. But in early 1970s Bretton Woods structure collapsed and massive structural changes to global economy emerged what Wayne Ellwood called, fundamentalist free market governments in Britain and US around 1980 and coupled with the disintegration of State run Command Economy in the erstwhile Soviet Union. The overall policy of the Thatcher administration as well as Regan administration was to reduce drastically the State regulatory role and enhance the operational and mobility powers of Private Companies. Free trade, unfettered investment, deregulation, balanced budgets, low inflation, and privatization of publicly owned enterprises were trumpeted as the six-step plan to national prosperity. This economic dimension of globalisation consists of drastic reduction of State regulatory roles, privatization, trade liberalization and more power to corporate bodies like TNCs and MNCs.

Cultural Dimension

Cultural dimension of Globalisation is also equally important because there is a close relationship between the two. Cultural globalisation means free exchange of cultural groups among all countries and free flows of cultural goods and commodities. It usually refers to the homogenizing process of global culture towards Western, particularly American Culture. It is due to this fact that globalisation is often considered as Americanization or Westernization and it is true to a great extent because there is a tendency of following West among the people across the globe.

Linking the Two Dimensions

It will be interesting to find out the symbiotic relationship between economic and cultural globalisation, which signifies the free flow of Cultural goods. Gramscian Cultural Hegemony (domination) is very much relevant in this context. In order to make people supportive of Capitalist Path of development and liberal democracy as a system of governance, minds of people across the globe have to be colonized, indoctrinated and make them convince of the superiority of a particular culture and mode of development. The influence of liberal Capitalist's ideology over the people is so strong and formidable that even the geographical division between East and West becomes irrelevant and today we find the 'West' in the 'East'. Thus the term Western has a cultural notion depicting a particular pattern of living and mode of thought. The cultural globalisation is so inextricably related to the Western that the former is portrayed as a product of the latter since for the sustenance of the free market economy, which favors and benefits certain highly industrialized Countries it is necessary to impart values that suits the system.

Emphasis given to negative liberty, individualism, consumerism, efficiency, innovation, rationality and productivity by the supporters of liberalization, privatization and globalisation (LPG) is also to be seen from this perspective. Besides this, other non western people are constantly made to believe that liberal capitalist path of development and its associated living patterns and thought culture is historically inevitable, absolute and there is no alternative. People living in the backward countries are constantly *bombarded* with this notion of historical inevitability. Daniel Bell's *End of Ideology,* Walt W. Rostow's *Stages of Growth* and Francis Fakuyama's *End of History* (which was all written in the backdrop of Soviet Union's breakdown), all beat the drums of Capitalist victory and indicate the liberal democracy as the ultimate.

Cultural Interaction and Globalisation

Globalisation in short has brought a radical transformation in the pattern of living across the globe. The constant and relentless flows of cultural commodities like goods, information, ideas, habits etc. indicate apparent interactions amongst the cultures. However behind this apparent façade of "cultural interactions", there is a reality of cultural superimposition which has resulted into the emergence of a number of resistance movements whose objectives are to defend and protect their own distinct cultures. It may not be wrong to say that globalisation is a top-down process. Therefore every aspect of globalisation is designed, shaped and patterned at the top according to the interests of the major actors of the market.

So the notion of cultural interaction cannot be applied at all levels. It may be true of some cultures which are large enough to compete with the invading western cultural images but for a small cultural group like ours the notion of cultural interaction will be a misnomer because interaction not only involves two cultures but also impact that each culture gives to one another. In this context it is difficult to locate what impact that our culture gives to ever invading global culture of consumerism, individualism and other images which are manufactured in the laboratory of the multi-national companies and the west and transmitted across the globe through information technology. And their influences upon the non-westerns who have distinct way of living are so profound and formidable that they accept it as inevitable and the best.

Globalisation is a top down process whereby it has sought to destroy the notion of collectivism, more so, the collectivity which politically and culturally means state intervention in the allocation and distribution of scarce resources for common good, social equity etc. The present phase of globalisation have attacked even the capitalist economies whose economic organizations function based on behavior dispositions other than the principles of laissez-faire. For example, the three salient features of Japanese system of economic organization are: 1. Lifelong rather than highly mobile employment relationship; 2. Long term, obligated, rather than auction market mobile supplier relations; and 3. Patient, long-term committed, rather than short term, return sensitive, equity capital and consequent absence of takeovers (Collin Crouch and Wolfgang Streek (eds), *Political Economy of Modern capitalism*). The three dimensions of difference of behavioral dispositions between the Japanese and Anglo-Saxon society are: 1. The Anglo-Saxons behave in ways designed to keep their options open-to keep their freedom to change jobs and loyalties, to shift investments as soon as the prospect of advantage occurs. Japanese are much more willing to foreclose their option by making long-term commitments from which, they accept; they can only disengage themselves with great difficulty. 2. In making their choices, Anglo-Saxons give greater weight to their own immediate welfare or that of their family or personnel friends. Japanese are much more likely, by virtue of their long-term commitments, to have diffuse obligations to promote the welfare of others- the other members of the firms they have joined, their partners in the long term trading relationships. Put starkly, this is a difference in the selfishness/ altruism dimension. 3. The third difference in behavioral dispositions is rather more made into an explicit cultural ideal than the previous two- a difference in the evaluation, and hence in the willingness to undertake, different kinds of economic activity. In Japan, producing goods and services, which directly enhance the lives of others, is good. Spending one's life in the speculative purchase and sale of financial claims is bad (*ibid.*).The present day Globalisation based on "Washington Consensus" of fiscal austerity, privatization and market liberalization is asserting the Anglo-Saxon behaviour as the Universal truth and even seeking the demise of Japanese model. The "Cultural Power" of the Anglo-Saxons seeks to destroy the notions of collectivity which restricts the freedom of the finance Capital, especially that of the Anglo-Saxon Finance Capital. The present day globalisation is antithetical to the notion of collectivity and hence it is all out to destroy values and behaviour dispositions, which are based on the notion of collectivity.

Manipur Context

To define culture briefly, Ralph Linton (1991) states that "The culture of a society is the way of life of its members, the collection of ideas and habits which they learn, share and transmit from generation to generation." In Clyde Klukhohn's elegant phrase, "Culture is the design of living held by members of a particular society". It defines the accepted ways of behaving of members of a particular society. Culture is the way the society organizes its institutions and shapes the behavior dispositions of the members of the society.

Various social institutions in Manipur were organized on the basis of collectivity. Collectivity, rather than individualism was the norm of the society. The Kingdom got precedence over the village, village over a family and family over an individual. This is well reflected in the old saying, "A village can be sacrificed to save a kingdom, a family to save a village and an individual to save a family". The economic institutions based on the notion of collectivity pervaded all walks of life.

Cooperation rather than competition was the basis of interaction.

Western liberal education brought many things with it and individualism was also one of the notions it brought along with. So, the individual excellence is encouraged, whereas working for a collective interest is discouraged. The welfare of an individual rested with the welfare of the collectivity as a whole in the past, whereas, the welfare of the collectivity now lies with the welfare of an individual. *Mine first and society second is the motto*. These changes in the behavioral dispositions have been witnessed amongst a large section of people especially the urbanites in the last many years. The strongest attack to the collectivity, organized traditionally also came from the various institutions promoted by the State. There has been a superimposition of institutions with regards to the traditionally organized institutions and state promoted institutions are concerned. Yet the notion of collectivity is still present in various social institutions. The organization of Clubs in all the localities of Manipur in hill as well as plain integrates the democracy with the notion of collectivism. The people of Manipur still manage to sustain the traditional institutions of collectivity at the village and local levels. Though the cooperation and participation to these institutions have been reduced very much, the traditional and religious sanction for the existence of such institutions still exists. The behavioral dispositions towards collectivity is well reflected when the people as a whole is responding to some perceived threats to the society. Many people participate in the various movements in Manipur because of a sense of collective participation.

Having said all this, Globalisation is definitely attacking the already eroded notion of collectivity. It is now a three-way interaction. Forces derived from traditional authority, State and Market now interact to give what is so called Globalisation and Cultural Interactions in Manipur. Globalisation, deriving its legitimacy from the market forces and supported by the Cultural Power of the Anglo-Saxons is definitely for individualism and privatization. And as such the force of globalisation acts against the notion of collectivity and encourage various behavioral dispositions, which are basically individualistic and beneficial to develop the so-called Market Forces. The Forces generated by the tradition is weak to sustain the already eroding values and notions of collectivity, which derive its legitimacy from it. The State, while effecting the erosion of the traditional institutions, could not build the legitimacy for alternate institutions representing the values and notion of Collectivity. In fact it is now giving away the space it has gathered from tradition to the market forces represented by the Globalisation. But the values and notions of collectivity will have a strong and new supporter from the forces of resistance generated by the Globalisation itself. Hence the Globalisation and cultural interactions in Manipur will be in the form of a struggle between the values and notions of collectivity versus that of individualism.

REFERENCES

Ralph, E. Lerner, Robert Meacham, Standish and Mc Nall Burns, Edward et al., *World Civilisations*, Vol. 2, Eighth Edition, 1991. W.W. Norton & Co. Inc., New York.

Heywood Andrew, *Politics 2000*, Palgrave Publications.

Michie, Jonathan and Condon, F.D. (Ed.), *Encyclopedia of Social Science*, Vol 1. 2001, Chicago.

Ellywood, *No Nonsense Guide to Globalisation*, 2001, London,

Beck, Ulrich, *Risk Society Towards a New Modernity*, 1992, Sage Publications, New Delhi.

Collin Crouch, Wollgang Street, *Political Economy of Modern Capitalism*, Sage Publications, New Delhi.

10

Globalisation and Culture: Manipur Experience

—CHINGLEN MAISNAM

'Globalisation' is a very powerful and difficult word encompassing many aspects and meanings. "It is not simply about economics or even growing cultural and social interdependencies of the global village that drinks coke and watches Disney" writes Tabb (2002: 13) "'Globalisation' depicts a process of interconnectedness among states and societies". Thus, according to Bagchi (1997:21) "Globalisation means a much close-interaction between society, state and the market". It is generally believed that any nation that refuses to join the globalisation march will be left behind. As Ahmad (2003: 19) has correctly observed that the spread of globalisation "hits humanity like a hurricane, something entirely impersonal, driven by technology and finance which have escaped the control of every one, including actual nation-states, a force so powerful that any nation that refuses to join its drive shall be left behind".

Commenting on the economic and political characteristics of the present phase of globalisation, Castro (quoted in Surjeet 2001: 4) says, "the world is globalised, really globalised, a world dominated by the ideology, the standards and the principles of neo-liberal globalisation . . ." it is "nobody's whim: it not even anybody's invention . . . 'Globalisation' is a law of history. It is a consequence of the development of the productive forces". Though the globalisation has been going on since the beginning of history what we are witnessing today is only a new form of globalisation that has come fully into its own only within the last one and half decades or so. The present phase of globalisation is, to a great extent, based on 'Washington Consensus' which is also known as neo-liberalism or market fundamentalism [Mishra, 2003: 4]. John Williamson of International Institute of Development Economics, coined this term in 1990. These policies, according to Nobel Laureate Stiglitz (2003: 16) denoted a consensus between the IMF, the World Bank and the U.S. Treasury. A country going in for the Washington consensus-based globalisation will be beholden to the World Bank-IMF-WTO trinity for guidance [Mishra *op. cit.*: 4]. As is well known the market fundamentalists are always projecting market as sole option. They are also propagating de-politicisation of people and development [Amin, 2003: 9]. In order to reap benefits from the globalisation majority of the countries of the world including India dropped 'Command Economy' and adopted 'Market Economy'.

Now, the fundamental question is whether opportunities and benefits of globalisation among countries with different socio-economic and cultural setup are evenly distributed or not? In this connection World Bank in its World Development Report (2005) mentioned as follows:

- Nearly half the World's people still live on less than $ 2 a day and the 1.2 billion survive on less than $ 1 a day. [World Bank, 2005: 189]

  UNDP Human Development Reports 2003 and 2004 took serious note of the widening gap between the wealthy countries and periphery and disease's impact of the global development changes.

- Just as globalisation has systematically benefited some of the world's regions, it has bypassed others as well as many groups within countries [UNDP: 2003: 16].
- In 46 countries people are poorer today than in 1990. South Asia and Sub-Sahara are home to the largest countries of hungry people. Every 799 million people

in developing countries about 18% of the world's population – go hungry [UNDP, 2004: 132].

- About 900 million people belong to ethnic, religious, racial or linguistic groups face discrimination [*Ibid*., 129].
- Around the world, 42 million people are living with HIV/AIDS. The disease has already killed 22 million people and left 13 million orphans in its wake.[UNDP 2003: 41].
- Every year more than 10 million children die of preventable illness – 30,000 a day. More than 500,000 women a year die in pregnancy and childbirth. Diarrhoea is a major killer of young children; in the 1990s, it killed more children than the people lost to armed conflict since the World War II. [*Ibid*: 41]

An Indian Women's Organisation (AIDWA, 2002) remarks, "Globalisation is not gender neutral". It reports that:

- Women and children make up 70 per cent of the World's very poor. They provide 66 per cent of hours worked but receive only 10 per cent of the revenue and own only 1 per cent of property. Two-thirds of those deprived of literacy are women and two-thirds of children who do not go to school are girls.
- As far as labour standards are concerned, it is estimated that a women employed in Indonesia by U.S. MNC NIKE would have to work 1500 years to earn the equivalent of what an executive working in the U.S. would earn.
- One of the symbols of the globalised world is the fast growing sex tourism industry (also body shopping) and the trafficking of women and children with an annual turnover of several billion dollars. Over 2 million children are trafficked globally every year.

A cursory look at these few indicators have exposed the character of the present world order. The major part of the burden of this havoc is ultimately borne by those least able to bear it; the weak, the poor, the backward. Indeed, globalisation has not been kind to weak and disadvantage.

It empowers the rich and already strong. The result: of the 100 largest economies on the world, 52 are not countries; they are corporations [Albert, 2004: 23]. It has come to mean that globe belongs to rich and should continue to belong to the rich. [Mitra, 1997: 3]. Though it means market integration embodying a framework of deregulation, liberalisation and privatisation in the developed West (Mittleman, 2002: 2), it is the new synonym for imperialism and colonialism in the poor countries [Galbraith, 2002: 11].

The ongoing globalisation is America-led globalisation. That just as the previous phase of globalisation was under British hegemony, the current phase has to be under U.S. domination. McQual (2000: 221) has equated globalisation to Westernisation in general and Americanisation in particular. "Is globalisation a kind of political ethnocentrism which equates US = Universal ?" Jameeson (quoted in Viswanathan, 2001: 13) bluntly put it, "Is the US us?"

Globalisation has far reaching implications on culture. Here again the spread of Americanisation is quite evident. Sekar (2003: 38) says, "Globalistion is Americanisation. The attraction of the American way of life and culture is so powerful". ILO in its latest report has also concerned at the overwhelming dominance of the culture and values of the US and other Western Countries [ILO, 2004: 48-9]. Mishra (2003: 15) has rightly warned, "the world had no alternative but to accept American ideas, values and the way of life". Thus globalisation leads to cultural invasion.

Since globalisation has its own dominant culture it promotes homogenization of cultures, life style, consumption standards etc., as a consequence, we can visualize many changes in the life style of the people world over. If we look at the following facts and figures provided by UNDP (1998: 37) of the growth in consumption we could easily understand the priorities and direction of the world:

- Amount spent on cosmetics in the USA is $ 8 billion;
- Amount spent on ice cream in Europe is $ 11 billion;
- Amount spent on perfumes in Europe and US is $ 12 billion;

- Amount spent on pet foods in Europe and USA is $ 17 billion;
- Amount spent on cigarettes in Europe is $ 50 million;
- Amount spent on alcoholic drinks in Europe is $ 105 billion;
- Amount spent on Narcotic drugs in the world is $ 400 billions.

The above data provided by UNDP speaks of an "explosion" in consumption. A huge sum of money is wasted and burnt on non-essentials and wasteful and harmful expenses. Thus, productive investment is being diverted towards an extremely limited market for producing luxury consumption items instead of commodities of mass consumption. The concerns, the focus and the thrusts of official policies of the globalising third world countries have also undergone a dramatic change even in the official jargon. Prices of share markets are more important than prices of essential commodities, the provision of cellular telephones has greater priority than the provision of drinking water to teeming millions. Soft drinks are to receive higher priority over necessary food items, luxury cars over mass transport and software technology park over low cost latrines. It is the true character of the present global development which encourages elitist growth by which only a microscopic percentage of population is going to be benefited. As Stiglitz (2003: 20) has correctly pointed out, "the net effect of the policies set by the Washington Consensus has all too often been to benefit the few at the expense of the many, the well-off at the expense of the poor". Thus, globalisation unites the market and divides human beings [Ahmad, 2001: 23].

Another crucial aspect is the idea that culture can be identified and expressed in physical or other goods that can be traded and sold, such as crafts, films, books as well as music. Trade in international culture industry has become one of the largest and certainly the fastest growing in the world (Ghosh, 2000: 5), thanks to new technologies, such as satellite, television, multimedia and the Internet. Indeed, communication is the vehicle through which culture passed on from generation to generation, people to people and person to person [Pillai 2002:8]. According to UNDP (2004: 86, 183), world trade in cultural goods – cinema, photography, radio and television, printed matter, literature, music and visual arts – increased from $ 95 billion in 1980 to more than $ 380 billion in 1998. The number of television sets per thousand people worldwide was more than doubled from 113 in 1980 to 229 in 1995 and further to 243 since then. The world also witnesses the rapid spread of Telephone and cellular subscribers and Internet users. The Telephone mainlines increased from 81 per thousand in 1990 to 175 in 2002, cellular subscribers from 2 to 184 and Internet users from 0.5 to 99.4 in the same periods.

The world trade in culture particularly entertainment related areas is increasingly dominated by the U.S. Now, entertainment has become the single largest export industry of the U.S. The single most dramatic indicator of this is the film industry in which the global dominance of America is starker than even before [Ghosh, op.cit: 5]. The international dominance of US films is just one aspect of the spread of Western consumer culture. At the moment, US film productions regularly account for about 85% of film audiences worldwide. In the audiovisual trade with just the European Union, the US had a $ 8.1 billion surplus in 2000, divided equally between films and television rights.[UNDP 2004: 86]. In the production of film Titanic alone, they could earn a total gross revenue of US $ 1.8 billion of which $ 1.2 billion came from abroad [ibid: 109]. It may be noted that film is one of the powerful conveyors of life styles and carries social messages. It can have a powerful cultural impact. Thus, the possession of the technology becomes essential to be able to survive in the globalised world.

Manipur society also experiences the impact of ongoing neo-liberal globalisation where "every moment of existence is burdened by the frightening threat that the meaning of meaning is beyond our grasp" (Mitra, 2004: 3). In this very extremely complicated and complex situation, the people of this resource starved, crisis ridden and backward state of Manipur face extremely invasive technologies of globalisation in a way that colonial machineries never could have. The growth of a powerful international media enables the big economic powers of the world to directly intervene and influence social and cultural life of the people. Indeed, if we have the internet, we can be in much more intimate ad regular contact with some one living in Chicago than with someone else who lives at the other end of Churachandpur but does not have a phone. Every single middle class home in Manipur connected with the International TV channels has now become a classroom for promoting consumerist values. The values and tastes of the West are being superimposed on Manipur society. The local entertainment programmes increasingly reflect Western influence, not only in the content but even in the form and style of its presentation. A Beauty Contest, modeling and fashion shows have now found their place even in small towns of the state. Marketised version of beauty is taking place in this debt ridden and poverty-stricken state. It seeks to evaluate women mainly on the basis of her 'Looks'. In other words, body image has come to be seen as an indication of one's worth, identity and personality. Today women of Manipur have a growing concern for their skin, hair, body, colour, looks, weight curve and curl like their counterparts in the West. To argue on the lines of Mishra (2004: 8), "the entire interpretation of beauty gets sexualized. The preference for short-cut garments/clothes to expose the body without being completely nude, the passionate initiative to maintain an anorexic pattern of diet-intake and body weight, the investment to maintain a sexy, attractive body shape and size and remain continuously young without growing old despite one's chronological age". All these aspects explain a paradigm shift in the relation between beauty and identity. The homogenization of beauty is in fact consonance with 'globalisation'. It is interesting to note that the globalised wave of high voltage advertisement campaign has also reached in Manipur. Women have been used as an effective weapon for advertisement and entertainment like a commodity – a commodity that one can buy from the market as cosmetics. This has raised serious ethical questions on the status and position of women in society. The purveying of consumerist, egoist and descendent values intensified the tendency to look down upon the women of poor and deprived sections. Thus, the challenge is enormous.

The spread of aggressive market values, however has not replaced feudal ones, rather they have commercialized them. In this era of global competition, feudal cultures and habits still prevail upon the Manipur society. Wide illiteracy and lack of science consciousness prevail and superstition strongly rules. Even the media is highlighting the glory of superstition and supernaturalism. Healing services are available in local TV channels. Globalisation going on but consciousness not rising, it is an enigma, we have to find a solution! Watching Hollywood movies, wearing Nike shoes, drinking coke using cell phones on one hand and chanting mantras to the rising sun and performing *pujas* to the domestic animal for rain water. . . How a contrasting gape within a small society! One section of society using most sophisticated products of 21st century while others tilling their fields with the same tools which were used during the days of 33 AD. Is it not the case of what Freidman (2002) argued "One Country, Two Worlds".

It seems that the mindless cultural invasion of globalisation might jeopardize one day the exclusive identity and glorious heritage of Manipur society. The experiences show that there are ominous signs of distortion in cultural practices of both the tribal and non-tribal in the recent years due to the ongoing globalisation drive. This drive might inflict incalculable injury to one of the finest traditions and heritage of the land. So, we should ponder over this development to settle things in the right direction so that the rich culture and tradition of Manipur do not sweep away against the forces of inexorable time. The challenge is so enormous, but together and united we must and shall overcome the forces of darkness and destruction. As Sen (1999) has rightly pointed out that learning from each other is extremely important but our approach has to be critical. Much that is anachronistic in our own cultures shall have to be disregarded much that is progressive in foreign cultures must be made our own. A living culture must always have an orientation towards the future and must therefore look at its own past critically and skeptically. The draft culture policy of Manipur (GOM 2000:4) has also directly echoed the same view, it states. "The policy believes that while resisting colonization of minds, our culture should remain in constant dialogue with the world at large in the realm of ideas, perceptions, media and expressions". It needs to be noted here that we have to beware of the fundamentalist or communal or ethnic divisive ideology – who clearly mixes religion, culture and nationhood in the name of opposing western or the so called Indian culture. All efforts should be made to build a progressive forward looking culture for our people. We should not allow culture to become the privilege of the few. We should oppose mindless cultural invasion of globalisation. The progressive and forward looking people all over the world see the spread of globalisation as a force destroying people's culture because ongoing globalisation is one-way globalisation. Thus, there is an urgent need to evolve a alternative strategy to make the ongoing globalisation a two way process. Since the elite have lost the urge to evolve indigenous ideas, the people's interest stands sacrificed. Since the costs of one way globalisation for the people are mounting rapidly and reversal of policies is going to be more and more difficult as time elapses united voice and actions are called for. To quote Amin (2000:20) "The issue is not globalisation or withdrawing from the world and going to the moon. There are many alternatives". What we need today is another kind of globalisation that ushers the world in an equitable and human society. We are already late, let it not be too late.

REFERENCES

Ahmed, Aijaz (2001), "Culture and Globalisation", *Students Struggle*, 30(7), July 2001, pp.17-28.

Albert, Michael (2004), "What are we For?" *Students Struggle*.

Amin, Samir (2000), "Globalisation, Regionalism and Democracy: An Interview with Samir Amin", *Multinational Monitor*, April 2000, Vol.25, No.4.

Amin, Samir (2003), "Market and Religious Fundamentalisms Are Complementary", An interview with Semir Amin, *Peoples Democracy*, Vol. XXVII, No.2, Jan 6-12, 2003.

AIDWA (2002), *Perspectives, Interventions and Struggles* (1998-2001), All India Democratic Women's Association, New Delhi.

Barnet, Richard and John Caranagh (1996), "Homogenization of Global Culture" in Jerry Mander and Edward Goldsmith, eds.,

The Case Against Global Economy, pp.71-77, San Francisco: Scira Club Books.

Freidman, L. Thomas (2002), "One Country, Two Worlds" *The New York Times*, Jan. 28, 2002.

Galbraith, James, K. (2002), "A Perfect Crime: Inequality in the Use of Globalisation", *Daedalus* Winter 2002, pp.11-25.

Ghosh, Jayati (2000), "Globalisation and Culture", *Souvenir*, 10, All India Conference of SFI, Jan. 2000.

Government of Manipur (2002), *Manipur Culture Policy (A Draft)*, Deptt. of Art & Culture, GOM, Nov. 2002.

ILO (2004), *World Employment Trend*, Geneva: International Labour Organization.

Leiven, Anatol (2004), "In the Mirror of Europe: The Perils of American Nationalism", *Current History*, pp.99-106, March 2004, Vol. 103, No.671.

Murthy, Goutam (2003), "Globalisation in the Economic Reforms period of the Indian Economy" in Dr. Y. Suguna, Dr. G. Rama Krishna, Dr. A.G. Moss (eds.), *Economic Reforms in India: Retrospect and Prospect*, pp.389-398, Mumbai: Himalaya Publishing House.

Mittelman, James, H. (2002)"Globalisation: An Ascendant Paradigm?", *International Studies Prospective*, No.3, pp.1-14.

Mishra, Girish (2003), "Globalisation and Cultures: Some Aspects", *Mainstream*, Vol.XLI, No.35, Aug 16, 2003, pp.15-18.

Mitra, Ashok (1997), "Inaugural Speech to a Students' Conference", *Students Struggle*, Vol. No.3, June, 1987, p.3.

Mitra, Ashok (2004), "The Seige of Inauguration", *Social Scientist*, 376-377, Vol.32, No.9-10 Sept. Oct., 2004, pp.3-6.

Pillai, P. Govinda (2002), "Globalisation and Culture", *Peoples Democracy*, Vol.XXVI, No.1 Dec. 31- Jan.6.

Sekar, I., Francies Gnana (2003), "Impact or Globalisation on Indian Culture", *Third Concept*, Vol.17 No.196, June 2003, pp.37-40.

Sen, Amartya (1999), "Our culture, ethnic culture", *West Bengal, A West Bengal Govt. Fortnightly*, Vol.XLI No.1-2, Jan 1-16, 1999.

Stiglitz, Joseph, (2003), *Globalisation and Its Descendents,* New Delhi: Penguin Books.

Surjeet, H.K. (2001), "Globalisation and Liberalisation, Its Impact on State, Social and Cultural Aspects", *Marxist*.

UNDP (1998), *Human Development Report 1998.*

UNDP (2003), *Human Development Report 2003.*

UNDP (2004), *Human Development Report 2004.*

Visvanathan, Shiv (2001), "The Problem", *Seminar Globalisation*, 503, July 2001, pp.12-13.

World Bank (2005), *World Development Report 2005*, The World Bank, Washington D.C., 2004, p. 189.

11

Regional Formulation of Islam in Manipur

—SYED AHMED

[ABSTRACT

The overhiarching theme of this paper is to reconstruct the socio-cultural aspects of the Muslims in Manipur. To this end, an analysis of the cultural accretions and influences from the local environment since the dawn of their history in Manipur, which serves as a paradigm for the regional formulation of Islam, is made. And along with it the genesis and evolution of the movement to 'cleanse' the non-Islamic accretions from the Muslim folks and instead instil in them a purer form of faith is traced and examined.]

Introduction

As against the polemical and didactic writings of traditional Islamic scholars – that upheld Islam as a homogeneous mass of a religious and cultural uniformity[1] - modern researches have shown that "underlying the creedal, doctrinal, and ritualistic unity in Islam, the Muslim world, at the micro-level, presents a much more complex reality of unquestioned pluralism and diversity."[2] Islam, therefore, is not only an ideology, but it is also a cultural system. This cultural system has two sets of representations. Firstly, those cultural values that are rooted in certain Islamic beliefs and concepts, which are universal and constant across regions or territories. For example, Muslims throughout the world share the five cardinal pillars of faith viz., the *shahada,* or creed (acknowledgement of the oneness of God and the prophethood of Muhammad), *salat*, or prayer, fasting (*ramzan*), *zakat* (alms to the poor), and *hajj* (pilgrimage to Mecca). Secondly, there are those cultural values, which are essentially social in character, and are accretions from the regional culture, in which a particular Muslim group exists. And this culture differs from region to region. These cultural accretions are usually manifested through dress, food, language, literature, life-cycle rituals, social structure, beliefs in the supernatural, arts and aesthetics, etc. Such cultural values developed as a response to diverse cultural situations to which Islam had to adapt and adjust as it made its course from the West Asian heartland to the diverse parts of the world. The Muslims adapted these new cultural values to their own requirements and needs by putting an Islamic tinge into it.[3]

In the Indian sub-continent too, comprehensive studies have shown that besides the universally ordained Islamic laws, Islam as practiced by its adherents is overlaid with elements which are accretions drawn from the local environment.[4] One of the main agents that led to the development of such cultural values were the converts, who carried with them into their new faith, values and practices of their original environment.[5]

It is noteworthy that many rituals and practices also came from outside India with the Islamic faith e.g. veneration of Muslim saints and their *dargahs*. These were picked up in the course of Islam's journey through the vast areas of Asia and Africa. The Islamic traditions and the indigenous and exotic custom-oriented traditions intermingled to such an extent that they became complementary and essential part of a single religious system. Such ritual practices and beliefs may not be orthodox and thus condemned by the *ulemas* (Islamic scholars) and reformers, but they remain hard to be ignored or crushed. It persists and functions for those who believe in it, and serves some 'practical needs', which the religion does not provide.

The sociocultural aspects of the Muslims in Manipur are no exception. Here too, Muslim and Islam made mutual adjustments at various levels with the local environment thereby practicing syncretistic beliefs and practices. Many of these local elements could be seen in the realm of language, food, dress, habitation pattern, social organization, life-cycle rituals, festivities, arts and aesthetics, and beliefs and behavioural patterns, which could be described as 'practical religion', etc. This practical religion includes supernatural theories of disease causation, e.g. phenomena such as spirit possession, evil eye, etc., and their remedial measures through charms and sorcery, to mention a few.

Muslims in Manipur

Muslims, locally referred to as *Pangals*, are the third largest religious community in Manipur, constituting 6.9 per cent (as per 2001 Census) of the total population.[6] Their history in the region—some 400 years old—is traced from the reign of Khagemba (A.D. 1597-1652), who made a thousand Sylheti Muslim soldiers, engaged by one of his step-brother to seize the throne. Muslim population was strengthened in due course of time by Muslim immigrants, in small number, from Sylhet, Tripura, Assam, Bengal, and other parts of mainland India. Later, owing to the recognition of their skills and efficacy they were persuaded to settle in the valley by offering local girls in marriage and granting lands.[7]

Cultural Synthesis

In due course of time, Muslims underwent many adjustments and modifications in their socio-cultural aspects. They adopted various local traits according to their own requirements and needs by putting an Islamic content into the traits. Thus the Muslims in Manipur accepted *meiteilon* as their mother-tongue. They imbibed the local diet, costume, and habitation pattern of the region. In fact, the climatic and physical environment of a region determines these traits. Local accretions and excrescences in some of the select socio-cultural aspects of the Muslims in Manipur are discussed below.

Social Stratification

Islam, in principal, does not permit the segregation of its followers into any hierarchical divisions. The only measure of status in Islam is piety, not power, position, profession, or wealth. But, in spite of the theoretical equality, Muslims of the sub-continent practice and follow an inbuilt caste system, corresponding, to some extent, to those of the Hindus. Administrative records dating back to the middle of the 19th century, recent works on social history, and several other anthropological studies on the Indian Muslim societies suggest the presence of caste-like features among the Muslims in different parts of India. And it made inroads, to a large extent, into the Indian Muslim society with the induction of converts, especially those from the intermediate and lower rungs of the Hindu society; wherein status is strictly defined in terms of birth and maintained by strong sanctions.[8]

An almost similar caste-like social division is in vogue amongst the Muslims of Manipur. However, these divisions, unlike in other parts, are very vague and not hierarchical and it has, therefore, no bearing on the social relations amongst them. For instance, the clan *Merai* is regarded as *Sayyid*; clans like *Moijing*, *Chesam*, *Dolaipabam*, *Phisbam*, *Bogi, Phusam* are regarded as *Sheikhs*; and clans such as *Epham, Kazikhut, Panjaimayum, Yumkham* are regarded as *Pathans*.[9]

Instead Muslims in Manipur give more importance to their clans, which they have adopted from their immediate neighbour, the *Meities*. They have also imbibed some of its related ideology and practices. For instance, it regulates marriage and kinship. Shortly after their settlement, the rulers of Manipur gave family titles to the Muslims on the basis of the specific occupation they perform, their place of settlement and origin, etc. The family title so awarded to a man had become the name of the clan or *sagei* of his lineage. Today there are around 50 Muslim clans in Manipur.[10]

Marriage Customs

As per the Islamic law, marriage is a purely civil contract; solemnize with certain verses from the *Quran* along with the signing of a legal document (*nikah-nama*). Interestingly, it does not prescribe any service peculiar to the institution or occasion. However, various sociological and anthropological studies on the sociocultural life of Muslims of India have shown the co-existence and interaction of the Islamic marriage customs and local non-Islamic customs, the latter subsequently become Islamised.[11]

The Muslims in Manipur also have adopted various marriage customs from the *Meiteis.* Muslims also, like the *Meities*, traditionally practice lineage or clan exogamy. Since all the members of the clan trace their descent from a common ancestor, marriage within the clan is considered to be an incestuous alliance. They practice elopement (*chenba*) as a popular way of acquiring mate, which is rarely practiced by their brethrens outside, over and above the practice of negotiation (*heinaba/thijaba*). Besides the *nikah* ceremony – prescribed by Islam for sealing a marital union between two persons – which is performed strictly according to Islamic rules, the Muslims in the region also adopt elaborate local marriage customs and rituals. As soon as a marriage is settled, the cycle of these ceremonies starts and continues until the actual performance of the marriage itself.

Muslims, like the *Meiteis,* perform an elaborate engagement ceremony, which consist: *mauthiba chungba* or *mangol kaba, kwa-khaiba*, *hajipot-puba*, *sagei kwa-chatpa*. Muslims usually follow the *Meitei* almanacs in deciding and fixing the date of marriage and other local beliefs associated with marriage.

We have been informed by the older generations that various forms of entertainment also formed part of the Muslim marriage in the past. They played *kangjei* (local version of hockey) and *mukna* (local version of wrestling) and sang *ghazals, kasidas* (panegyrics) *khullang esei.*[12]The bride also performed along with her close friends *thabal,* a traditional dance of the *Meities*, and *mairbag jagoi*, a unique dance form without music.[13] However, many of the local and un-Islamic marriage customs have discontinued over the years mainly due to the preaching of the *ulemas* and learned scholars, which is dealt in the subsequent paras. It is only recently that during Muslim marriage *sumang lilas* (dramas staged at the courtyard) were staged and loud speakers were used belting out latest songs from Hindi films.

Belief and Rituals

The Muslims in Manipur also adopt many other beliefs and behavioural patterns of local origin, which could be described and leveled as belonging to the realm of what is called 'practical religion'. These broadly include belief in the therapeutic (*karamat*) and intercession (with the creator) power of the Muslim *ulemas* (*bujurk*), faith in spirits and supernatural theories of disease causation, and belief in phenomena such as evil eye, spirit possession, etc., and their remedial through resort to sorcery, charms and magic; and beliefs and rituals practiced in the day-to-day life, e.g., those associated with parturition, death, agriculture, natural calamities, etc.

Charms and Magic

Even though Islam condemned the practice and belief in sorcery or magic (*simiya*), except those, which do not associate things with God. Muslims throughout practice it without much hesitation.[14] Manipuri Muslims also believe in sorcery and charms, and those who practice the trait are known as *Pangal Maiba*, like their counterparts, *Meitei Maibas*. Muslim *Maibas* adopt many local practices, which are grafted into the system prescribed in the *Quran* and the *Hadith* (Islamic traditions).

Muslim *Maibas,* like the *Meitei Maibas*, indulge in exorcism and offer magico-religious services for treating those possessed by spirits, madness, hysteria, and all sorts of physical ailments. Such afflictions are treated and cured through prayers, offerings, rituals, *mantras*, holy or wise sayings (aphorisms), sacrifices, physiotherapy, herbal potions, etc.

Muslim *Maibas* invoke spirits, especially *Jinns* (associated with Islamic tradition). They command the presence of *Jinns* and caused them to do anything, e.g., to establish friendship or enmity between two persons, to increase wealth, to treat certain ailments and possession, casting out of devils, to recover stolen goods, etc.[15] Muslims also believe in the existence of local malignant spirits, e.g. *Helois* (nymphs), *Bhuts, Leiren,* etc. and Muslim *Maibas* invoke divine assistance to get rid of the baneful influence of these spirits. Muslims also believe in the phenomenon of evil eye (*nazar/mihu chungba*).

Muslim *Maibas* also adopt physiotherapy method known as *pukshuba*, manipulation of the belly, for treating ailments related to stomach e.g. indigestion, flatulence, constipation, muscle pain, etc. They also have expertise in treating ailments with the local herbal folk medicine method.

The art of *Maiba* is handed down from generation to generation. However, it is not hereditary; usually one old practitioner teaches the art to one, whom he finds reliable. Even today when medical science has made much advancement people still value the age-old skill of the *Maibas.*[16]

Puritan Movement

In the late 19th and early part of 20th century, Muslims throughout the world experienced a significant change in their religious outlook. One of the important aspects of this outlook was the insistence for a purer form of faith through purificatory purging of non-Islamic accretions and excrescences that was hitherto prevalent among the Muslim folks.[17] This new outlook found expressions in the various movements like *Wahhabi, Deoband*, *Ahl-i-Hadis*, etc. in the 19th century and *Tabliqi Jamaat*, *Jamaat-i-Islami*, etc., in the 20th century.

These new Muslim reforming sects also made their appearance in the North-East India in the late 19th and early 20th century.[18] These sects emphasized on the absolute monotheism (*tawhid*), denied all acts implying polytheism (*shirk*), such as visiting tombs, and venerating saints and non-Muslim deities, belief in magic and incantations. They levelled these practices as *bidat* (innovation), and advocated a return to the original teachings of Islam as incorporated in the *Quran* and the *Hadith.*[19]

The reform movement had its impact amongst the Muslims of Manipur also. From the early part of 20th century a small number of Muslims started moving out for religious studies, thereby coming in contact with their brethrens outside for the first time. The first batch of *ulemas* from Manipur returned after the completion of their courses from the *Madrassas* of Meerut, Rampur, Lahore, Delhi, Dhaka, Cachar, etc. in the early part of 20th century.[20]

It was these few *ulemas* who took the burden of regenerating the true Islamic tradition in Manipur by cleansing the non-Islamic accretions widely practised by the Muslim folks. By the late 19th and early part of 20th century, they travelled from village to village to expound to the Muslim folks the pure precepts of Islam and their basic duties as adherents through *massaura* (discussion), *waz* and *nasihat* (lectures) and folk-songs (dealt separately in the subsequent paras). They introduced the Islamic dress code, manners and etiquettes, life-style, etc.

They also took the initiative of establishing Islamic seminaries or *madrassas.* The first *madrassa* was established at Lilong in 1907.[21] Since then there has been phenomenal growth of *madrassas* in Manipur. In 1920, *Madrassa Mazhar-uloom* was established at Mayang Imphal Bengoon. Another *madrassa*, *Madrassa Imdadul Islam* was founded at Khelakhong in Thoubal District in 1965. In 1978-79, *Azizia Madrassa*, a residential *madrassa* for girls (*talibat)* was established at Khumidok. The foundation of one of the biggest *madrassas* in Manipur, *Darul-Uloom,* was laid at Lilong in 1980. At present the *madrassa* has four branches and around 800 boarding and non-boarding *talbas* (students). Over the years numerous *Madrassas* have been established in every nook and corner of the Muslim dominated areas. All these *Madrassas* are managed by public subscription on monthly basis, *khairat* and *imdaad* [donation and contribution from the rich and affluent Muslims, over and above *zakaat* (alms)].

Tabaligh movement took its root in Manipur from the 1960s. The movement is intended at creating a sense of community solidarity and religiosity by exhorting their followers to imbibe the letter and spirit of the *Quran* and the *Hadith*, and to follow the standards of an ideal life set by the Prophet and his companions, and work for the realization of an Islamic ideal.[22] It was the *ulemas*, learned scholars and *talbas* associated with *Deoband Madrassa* and *awam* (common people) that took the lead in this movement. The *madrassa* is also the *markaz* (headquarter) of *Tablighi Jamaat.* The *Jamaatis* travel from village to village (*safr*) preaching these ideals to their brethrens. They held *ijtima* or religious conference annually. The activities of *Jamatis* have broadened and intensified over the years. They are even going out of Manipur to preach.

Another important aspect in the movement for Islamic rejuvenation in Manipur is the publication of literatures by Muslim religious scholars in the vernacular on Islam and its basic tenets, obligations (*ahkams*), and the laws of the *Shariat* that operates in the daily life of the Muslims to bring mass awareness of the faith. These works make easy access of the religion to the mass that otherwise could not follow the works on Islamic tradition in the Arabic, Urdu and Persian languages. Even prominent stories from Islamic history and biography of Prophets are rendered in the vernaculars. Some of the prominent publications worth mention are: Munshi Ammanullah's *Punshiratki Pambai* (1924), Kazi Mujibur Rahman Rahi's *Hingnabagi Manngal* (1978), Muhammad Maneruddin's *Jannatki Leiteng* (1973), Haji Moulvi Helaluddin's *Punsigi Pambei* (1976), Moulvi Hatim Ali's *Hajrat Muhammad ki Punshi Wari* (1980), Abdur Rahman's *Yusuf Julekha* (1986), Kazi Mujibur Rahman's *Leila Majnu* (1994), Kayamuddin Pukhrimayum's *Alibabagi Wari* (1990), Muhammad Abdur Rahman's *Muharram Amasung Karbalagi Lal* (1992), to mention a few.

Further, to cater the sociocultural and religious needs of the Muslims a network of governmental and non-governmental organizations affiliated to national institutional bodies came up in Manipur. In 1961, *Jamiat-ul-Ulama*, an apex body of *ulemas* and a branch of the All India *Jamiat-ul-Ulema-i-Hind*, was instituted in Manipur. The *Jamiat* works for the propagation of Islam and its values; to secure and safeguard the religio-cultural, educational, and civil rights of the Muslims; to promote communal harmony in the state, etc. Manipur Wakf Board was constituted in 1988 to manage the *wakf* properties i.e., *masjids*, *madrassas*, *kabarstans* (common graveyards), etc., for religious and pious purposes, The Board also takes up various welfare schemes like providing financial assistance to the poor and the destitute, and scholarship to needy students, and grants for the promotion of technical and vocational skills. State Hajj Committee was also constituted to arrange and assist Muslims to perform *Hajj* at Saudi Arabia. Every year the committee sent hundreds of pilgrims. All these institutions and organizations help in organizing the socio-religious life of the Muslims systematically and smoothly.

Moreover, these institutions facilitate in linking up the community with their brethrens outside.

Marifat and Jang-nama

Folk songs served as an important medium for preaching and propagating Islamic precepts until the recent past. Mention must be made of two forms of folksongs – *marifat* (gnosis; literally meaning, special Islamic mystical knowledge) and *jang-nama* (war-ballads based on the Battle of Karbala). Both these types of folk songs form one of the most important oral traditions of the Muslims in Manipur. These songs were composed by *ulemas* and learned scholars mainly to remind the glory of God to Muslims in general, and especially to those who had strayed away from the virtuous path. The language used in composing the songs is simple and direct *meiteilon* with the tunes of *ghazals, qasidas* and *masnawis* set in harmony with the rural atmosphere of Manipur by employing indigenous themes and imagery. These songs were sung in groups on socio-religious occasions. It was sung usually at night at weddings ceremonies, community feast and at other social occasions.[23] So far no manuscript of *marifat* and *jang-nama* have been found. Muslims have instead orally transmitted these through generations, all these years. *Marifat* and *Jang-nama* are hardly sung these days. A specimen of an old popular *marifat:*

> Sollu pukningda illalla/Sollu pukninda allahu/Ningba thungdraba duniyani
>
> *Tumduna leiriba karigino / Akhiratki chengjel punaba laknasi*
>
> (Recite *Illalla* in your heart/Recite *Allahu* in your heart/This is a world of unfulfilled desires/ Why are you sleeping? /Let us prepare for the life after death.)

These songs made an attempt to provide the works on Islamic tradition in the Arabic and Persian in the vernacular to the illiterate Muslim folks. It was a bold step as it reduced the religious truth, enshrined in Arabic and Persian, to a 'profane' and earthy local language. They also attempted to set the Islamic characters, situations and stories in the natural geographical, social, and cultural environment of the land.

Summary

From the above study it has been observed that the socio-cultural aspects of the Muslims in Manipur presents a paradigm for the regional formulation of Islam. Even though Muslims in Manipur, like elsewhere in the Islamic world, believe in the cardinal pillars of their faith and its associated laws, their practical religion is overlaid with beliefs and practices that are accretions and influences from the local environment. These cultural values evolved gradually as a response to the existing cultural situations, adaptations and adjustments. The Muslims adapted these new cultural values to their own requirements and needs by giving an Islamic colour to it. In spite of the relentless preaching by the Muslim religious reformers from the early part of the 20th century up till date the Muslims fail to shed wholly the un-Islamic and local accretions and excrescences. Even today, if a child cries persistently at night, it is believed that a benign spirit possesses the child, and a *Maiba* is sought to cast off the spirit. In fact, the preachers, so far, fail to perceive that these local beliefs and practices, to a large extent, serve some 'practical needs,' which their religion does not offer. However, scholars have difference of opinion on this issue. One school of thought led by Aziz Ahmad and Clifford Greetz, believes that these folk and syncretic elements are temporary anomalies which eventually be eliminated by the Muslim reformers. On the other hand, another school of thought led by Imtiyaz Ahmad, M. Mujeeb, Mushirul Hasan, and others believe that syncretic (heterodox, heteroprax little tradition) and Islamic (orthodox, orthoprax great tradition) elements co-exist as complementary and integral parts of single common religious system.[24]

NOTES

1. In the Indian context almost all the medieval Islamic writers share this stance.
2. Asim Roy, *Islam in South Asia: A Regional Perspective*, New Delhi: South Asian Publication, 1996, p. vii.
3. See, for instance, Anwar Moazzam, "Islam/Muslim Culture(s): A Study of Relationship between Uniformity and Variety," *Islamic Culture* (Jan. 1979); Imtiyaz Ahmad (ed.), *Ritual and*

Religion Among Muslims in India, New Delhi: Manohar Publications, 1981, p. 15.

4. Mrs. Meer Hasan Ali's *Observations on the Mussulmauns of India* (1917) and Jafer Sharif's *Qanun-i-Islam* (Islam in India) are the earliest works which deals extensively on such beliefs and practices prevalent among the Indian Muslims. See also Imtiyaz Ahmad (ed.), *Ritual and Religion Among Muslims in India* and *Family, Kinship and Marriage Among Muslims in India*; New Delhi: Manohar Publications, 1976; Asim Roy, *The Islamic Syncretistic Tradition in Bengal,* New Delhi: Sterling Publishers Pvt. Ltd., 1993.
5. W. Crooke (ed.), *Islam in India*, Delhi: Low Price Publications, (1921) Reprint 1997, p. 9
6. *Census of India 2001,* Primary Census Abstract, Manipur, Registrar General of India.
7. L. Iboongohal and N. Khelchandra (ed.), *Cheitharol Kumbaba*, Imphal: Manipur Sahitya Parishad, 1989, p. 33; O. Bhogeshor and M.A. Janab Khan (ed.), *Nongsamei*, Imphal: Manipur Stationary and Printing Industries, 1973, pp. 1-7; R.K. Sanahal Singh, *Pangal Thorakpa*, Imphal: Liberty Publication Assn., 1990, p.5.
8. See, for instance, W. Crooke (ed.), *op. cit.,* p. 9; H. Risley, *The Imperial Gazetteer of India*, vol. I, New Delhi: Today and Tommorow's Printers and Publications, 1974, p. 329; Rouben Levy, *The Social Structure of Islam*, New York: Cambridge University Press, 1969, pp. 72-73; Zillur Khan, "Caste and Muslim Personality in India and Pakistan," *Man in India*, vol. 48, 2 (Jan.–Mar. 1968); Uma Guha, "Caste Among Rural Bengali Muslims," *Man in India,* vol. 45, 2 (1965); Imtiaz Ahmad (ed.), *Caste and Stratification Among Muslims in India*; Delhi: Manohar Book Service, 1973; J.H. Hutton, *Caste in India,* London: OUP, 1969, p. 2.
9. For a complete list of this stratification, see *Nongsamei, op. cit.,* pp.169-170.
10. For a detailed account of the origin of each of the Muslim clans, see Kulachandra Sharma and Badruddin, *Meitei-Pangal Haorakpham,* Imphal: Ching-Tam Press, 1981.
11. W. Crooke (ed.), *op. cit.,* pp. 56-88; Imtiyaz Ahmad (ed.), *Family, Kinship and Marriage Among Muslims in India*; New Delhi: Manohar Publications, 1976; Irshad Ali, "Marriage Among the Assamese Muslims," in S.M. Dubey's *North-East India—A Sociological Study*, pp. 117-120.

12. Also see Md. Riyazuddin Choudhury, "Folklore of the Muslims of Manipur," *Folklore* (June 1982), p. 121.
13. Md. A. Rahman and Md. Kayamuddin, *Pangal gi Khullang Esei* (Folksongs of Manipur Muslims), Imphal: Liberty Publication Assn., 1986, pp. 2-4.
14. For details, see W. Crooke (ed.), *op. cit.*, pp. 218-77.
15. See H.A.R. Gibb and J.H. Kramers (eds.), *Shorter Encyclopaedia of Islam.* Leyden: E. J. Briggs, 1961.
16. All the information on the skill and practice of the *Pangal Maiba* has been provided by Abdul Kadir, himself a *Maiba*, from Heibong Makhong, in Thoubal District.
17. Francis Robinson, *Islam and Muslim History in South Asia*, New Delhi: OUP, 2000, pp. 106-07.
18. B. C. Allen, *Census of Assam, 1901*, vol. II, Delhi: Manas Publications, 1984, pp. 8-9; W.W. Hunter, *A Statistical Account of Bengal*, vol. VI, Delhi: D.K. Publications, 1973, p. 383.
19. W.W. Hunter, *A Statistical Account of Bengal*, vol. VII, p. 222.
20. B. C. Allen. *Naga Hills and Manipur Socio- Economic History*, Delhi: (1905) Reprint 1980, p. 58; Kullachandra Sharma and Badruddin, *op. cit.*, pp. 148-49.
21. *Administrative Report of Manipur State for the Year, 1907-08,* National Archive of India; Kullachandra Sharma and Badruddin, *op. cit.,* pp. 148-49.
22. For details, see Moulana Wahiduddin Khan, *Tabligh Movement*, New Delhi, 1986.
23. Md. Riyazuddin Choudhury, *op. cit.,* p. 122.
24. For a discussion, see Francis Robinson, *op. cit.*, pp. 44-46.

12

Religious Movements and Cultural Synthesis in Manipur: An Observation on Manipuri Hinduism[1]

—N. VIJAYLAKSHMI BRARA

The Meitei Belief System

The origin

Atingkok (Father void), the infinite expanse, which embraces all within him and *Amamba*, the supreme infinite darkness, combined into *One*, are the starting points of all manifestations. They are the expressions of the ultimate reality. When these two manifestations combine into one the whole process of generation takes place. They are primal and external and cannot be consumed by even the devastation of fire at the end of *Chak* (time). Time appears to be real in the world of manifestations. When all disappears into the Supreme One, there is no manifestation, no space, as all are within Him.

Atingkok is the originator of all the seven Meitei *salais* (*loosely* termed as clans). Meitei belief about their social structure starts from the origin of the origins, from the combination of the two opposite forces – the life-giving source and the all-pervasive darkness/nothingness. The basis of their social structure rests on the belief in the cyclical concept of their origin. The process of coming out and then returning to this entity is the universal process of life, death, and rebirth of all things and beings, divine or human. Later, with the formation of the composite Meitei society these attributes were given to Pakhangba (the ancestor of Mangang/Ningthouja Salai), whose motif of a dragon with the tail in its mouth, symbolized that the universe starts and ends with him.

In order to create the world of living beings, Atingkok manifested himself in the form of two beings. His right side became Atiya Sidaba (the Sky God) and his left became Leimaren Sidabi (the Mother Earth/Malem). They became the Supreme *Pa* (father) and *Pi* (mother) for the whole world, the supreme male and female principles. In the Meitei social space, the right side is assigned to the males while the left side is assigned to females. The abode of these two manifestations is at the Koubru hills, which is also considered to be the place of origin of the Meiteis.

Awang Koubru Ashuppa
Laiyam Khunda Ahanba
Sanalik Mapal Thadringei
Sanalik Mapal Thariba
Nongthrei Mawoo Lingdringei
Nongthrei Mawoo Lingliba,

is a song describing the reverence people have for this hill. It means, 'Koubru peak to the north is the highest place where gods made their foremost habitation, and created different orders of living beings, Gods are the roots from which living beings bloom like flowers.

The 'world' is Meitei belief covers the vertical as well as horizontal space. Heaven is as much the part of the Creation as earth is and so are the other animate and inanimate things.

A human being is called '*Mee*', since it has been created in the pattern of *mi* (the shadow image), and the human body is a place of divine habitation.

Every time a child is born into this world, it is believed that *Atiya Sidaba* pierces into its body through the *Linju* (the top most, soft part of the head called the cortex) and takes in the five deities along with his breath. They are placed in the five parts of the body; *Koubru* settles in the cortex, *Marjing* in the heart, *Amamba* in the navel, *Thangjing* below the navel and *Wangpurel* in the genital organs. In this way all the deities of different directions in the physical world, protect the human being by placing themselves in all the vital parts of his body. The sixth soul, called *mi* (shadow) is part of the personality and is associated with the body at the time of birth. When the mid-wife (*maibi*) cuts the umbilical cord with a bamboo knife, she invokes all the six souls to take their place in the child.

Hence the image of the whole cosmos outside has a direct replica of it inside every human body. Every human thus represents a complete creation. And each creation of the outside world also shares a relationship of homology to a corresponding part of the human body.

The Cultural Interaction

The Meitei kings from early times had been mobile and interactive with other regions. War as well as trade had been a consistent feature of their relations with Burma (now Myanmar). The mythical animals called *Kangla Sha*, which became the royal symbols, are believed to have been built by the Chinese. Sericulture, and the brick-making techniques were also believed to have been brought by the Chinese.

In the post-Hindu era, Manipur came in closer contact-with the Ahom Kingdom of Assam and other neighbouring kingdoms of Tripura, Cooch-Bihar, Sylhet etc. Matrimonial and military alliances were forged with them.

These kinds of interactions enabled the Meitei society to develop its unique state apparatus, enrich its economy and widen the field of cultural contact.

The people of the hills by contrast, due to the hostile nature of their terrain were not able to have similar interactions with other societies.

In the course of time, two dissimilar societies emerged, a homogeneous and complex Meitei Society, and on the other hand various heterogeneous, scattered tribal societies. These two groups were further alienated when Hindu *Vaishnavism* invaded Manipur during the reign of King Charairongba, in the seventeenth century and made Meitei part of the pan-

Vaishnav culture. This alienation was further aggravated when the hill people adopted Christianity in the early part of the nineteenth century. By this time orthodox Hinduism was firmly entrenched in the Meitei society. It may be relevant to mention here that with the advent of Christianity, the traditional belief systems, that had provided the hill people with a link, albeit tenuous, with Meitei society, ended. The new religion discouraged the hill people from observing their traditional ceremonies and festivals as they were considered by the preachers of Christianity to be 'paganistic and primitive'. The rich culture and traditions of the hill people became relics of the past. Their role in shaping the present and future of the people were denied. Though it did not pose any challenge to the dominant Meitei society, the latter refused to acknowledge the new and alien religion. The 'new' way of life of the Christian hill people was ignored by the dominant Meitei society. Thus a big chasm was created between the hill and valley people.

The Cultural Theoretical Constructs

There are some theorists who believe that many social scientists while specifically studying the structural patterns of authority have tended to ignore the cultural component. I being one of them believe, that this element should form the basic premise if we are to understand the socio-political ethos of any society. Myths, legends, folklore, and festivals form very important areas for studying a society's state structure. They either glorify or mystify the king or, when a king is unpopular, they tell the story of his punishment, or of how he ought to have been pushed. A.M. Hocart goes as far as to say that:

> "The ritual organization is vastly older than government ..... . the functions now discharged by the king , prime minister, treasury, public works, etc., are not the original ones ... they were originally part, not of a system of government, but of an organization to promote life, fertility, prosperity by transferring life from objects abounding in it to objects deficient in it. Only gradually has the scope of this organisation become enlarged, and

its functions modified, until it has become a centralized means of organizing the activities of society."[2]

He proposes that rituals should form the basic premise to study a state apparatus since ritual "exists where there is no government and where none is needed."[3]

Denouncing theories based purely on economic factors, Hocart says that this is a very small fragment of life, and the pursuit of wealth is not one that inspires much zeal for common good. "You cannot build a State on the narrow basis of prices and wages, but only on the widest cooperation of life. Ritual as long as it retains it's meaning, is a cooperation for life."[4]

In the course of development, the organization will need a remodelling in making of a commander of a people who obey by and large, the social groups that were once equal would then stand in a vertical line. Hocart calls the process centralization. With centralization there would be a process of specialization – or the selection of different individuals to perform different tasks.

Hocart refers to the king of advanced and large communities or the head of a small tribe as 'Principal' of the ritual. By this he means that he is considered the God or the saviors of earth sent by God. Two types of kings are distinguished – kings who include in their divinity the divinities of their chieftains, and kings who are God, and whose chieftains, consequently, are only a dimmer reflection of that god. The latter type is an example of monotheism. According to him monotheism, centralization, and moralization cluster together in the higher stages of development. With the growth of centralization, the role of the chieftains is not reduced by changed. They remain as important as ever, in fact they become the real masters of rituals and the state, but are no longer in charge of things, even while they remain responsible for maintaining society.

Following Hocart's emphasis on ritual categories, Clifford Geertz builds a broader framework by emphasizing the need to study the whole cultural framework for development of the concept of a state.

The term state, according to Geertz, has at least three etymological themes condensed within it; **status**, in the sense of rank standing (the glories of blood and the state); **pomp** in the sense of splendour and display; and **governance**, in the sense of regency and regime. The third element to the exclusion of the other two has come to dominate modern political discourse. Such an approach does not fully explicate all the elements that constitute the concept of 'State'.

When we study a society through its cultural, cosmological, as well as political spheres, there is no need to mark it on an evolutionary scale, and nor do we need to arrange facts with the intention of creating generalized definitions. Instead, the nature of the state is understood by studying the perceptions, myths, and culture of that society. It then becomes a deep-rooted, contextual and complete understanding of the state structure beings studied. This approach recognizes the ethno-historical elements and unique cultural features particular to the society under study, instead of striving for a universal definition of state and its unilinear path of emergence.

According to Geertz's doctrine of '**exemplary centre**', which is basically a theory of the nature and basis of sovereignty, the court and capital are at once a microcosm of supernatural order – an image of the universe on a smaller scale and a material embodiment of political order. The ritual life of court is not only reflective of social order but also, and more so, of the supernatural order. The legitimization of this system is done by the means of myths.

Kangla, the capital, for Manipur kings was similarly a reflection of cosmic power. It was and is still believed to be the life - source, the naval of the whole state. The mythical king Pakhangba was and is still believed to be resting in the center of this capital. The court ceremonies, such as those of coronation, were at once an embodiment of the conjugation of the divine male and female principle, and a symbol of the proclamation of a prosperous state. Copulation between the king and his queen reflected the procreation of cosmic energies and also enhanced the procreative power of its people and its earth.

In Negara (the Balinese kingdom studied by Geertz), as in the case of Manipur, the major institution of political life was kingship. In this context attributing the divine right theory would not be incorrect, but perhaps, insufficient. The context of divinity and the popular perceptions of the king should also be studied. It is important, according to Geertz, to study how these characteristics emerged, how they were materially produced. It is here that the analysis of various myths relating to the concept of kingship becomes important. Individual kings come and go, but what they represent – the conception of order, the reflection of the divine – remains unaltered. "The driving aim of higher politics is to construct a state by constructing a king. The more consummate the king, the more exemplary the center. The more exemplary the center, the more actual the realm."[5]

The Vaishnava Touch

Most people's talk of the emergence of a composite society, characterized by an organized and planned administration, only from the time of King Garibniwaz, also known by the name of Pamheiba (AD 1709-1748). The reason for remembering no further into the past than the time of Garibniwaz, could be, first of all, that this is not a very remote past, and is still fresh in the lore, not from personal anecdotes but repeated from the anecdotes passed down from their immediate forefathers. Secondly, Meitei society in Garibiwaz's time underwent a dramatic upheaval when he adopted and enforced Hinduism as the state religion. For the first time in the history of Manipur a king had enforced an extreme measure, and the people of Manipur for the first time felt traumatized with the suppression and oppression exercised by their own kind. He also changed the whole administrative structure, from a structure of federal units to complete centralized control, and the people who until then used to be nominated for different offices by the nobles, were removed, to give place to the relatives of the king.

These kinds of drastic political changes, accompanied by the imposition of a new religion, must have been events that could not be easily forgotten. It also marked the beginning of a whole new era, the Hindu era.

Myths portraying Bhagyachandra (1748-1752 reinstated in 1759-1782), as a great warrior as well as a devout believer in Krishna, were circulated widely and continue to be believed, till today. He was professed to have divine powers, where he could converse with Lord Krishna in his dreams. His supper human strength to tame even a wild elephant were some of the extraordinary qualities attributed to him. He was regarded as a 'true' king', with divine powers. A statue of King Bhagyachandra with his feet on a kneeling elephant installed at the center of the market area of the state capital symbolizes his power and glory.

The title of *Lainingthou* (god kind) was restored to him. If Garibniwaz was known for changing the state religion, and bringing in a centralized structure, Bhagyachandra came to be known as the pioneer of cultural renaissance who introduced the Raashlila and a completely new way of worship. Vaishnavism was firmly grounded in his era.

It is important to study people's perceptions of their past – historical as well as mythological. These perceptions come into focus when rites, ceremonies, or a social or moral rule needs justification, explanation, and sanctity. Such occasions serve a function of strengthening tradition. In constantly keeping this alive through its ritual enactments – which in repetition are kept afresh in people's minds – it also elevates people by tracing them back to a higher, better, divine, and supernatural reality. But only when we relate myths to the present, and through the present, understands its importance that we make the study contextually relevant. It is only through juxtaposition of synchronic – diachronic and static-dynamic that provides a complete picture of the society under study.

Meiteis started calling themselves Hindus from the eighteenth century onwards. They worship Radha-Krishna and celebrate with gaiety all the festivals related to the lives of this divine couple. In their rites of passage they have adopted the life cycle rituals of the Brahmins and added these to their already existing rituals. They have been given Kshatriya status in the caste hierarchy, which is the only element of the caste system present in this society apart from the Brahmins.

The Meitei Hinduism

If we go through the works on Hinduism, the inevitable trajectory traces the origin of the caste system, the different castes and the religious role of the rest of the castes in relation to the Brahmins and then the description of certain Brahmanical texts such as the Vedas, Puranas, Dharmashastra, etc. According to Lois Dumont the religious principle gets articulated in the Indian case in terms of the opposition of purity and impurity. For Dumont, as well as for Max Weber, the Brahmins represent the highest form of purity attainable by Hindus.[6] Whenever Hinduism is discussed it is, first of all, predominantly a Brahmanical view, (Dumont *et al.*) and secondly, it is always intrinsically premised on the caste system. Therefore, Hinduism and caste-system have become inseparable.

Caste, according to Weber, is about the imposition of ritual rights and duties and the position of Brahmins. It is the fundamental institution of Hinduism. "*Without caste there is no Hindu.*"[7]

However, a researcher with knowledge of Hinduism from such a perspective will find a different situation while studying the Meitei Hindus. The difference is born out of the fact that Hinduism in Manipur is not the base for the evolution of its social categories. The hierarchy of different strata does not correspond to the ascriptive hierarchy given in the caste system. The Brahmins came from Orissa, Bengal and other parts of India to spread the message of Hinduism. They are the late migrants who were given a place in the Meitei social structure under state patronage. Meiteis of all the seven *salais* converting to Hinduism were given Kshatriya status; people who did not convert were assigned the status of outcasts, the *Lois*. But the concept of untouchability assigned to the *Shudras(*the lowest in hierarchy in the caste system) could not make inroads in relation to the *Lois*. Nor could the hierarchy inherent in the caste system - Brahmins, Kshatriyas, Vaishyas, and Shudras (in that order) strike a parallel form in the Meitei social structure. In fact, hierarchy was based on the basis of royalty - the kingship principles, and that too was not rigid. People were the most important opinion makers and no king could rule without the consent of the people.

The division of labour in society was not based on birth, but on age and closeness to the king. Unlike the caste system, interaction at all levels was possible. At the base of *salai* structure was the rule of exogamy implying an equal status assigned to all of them. This was perhaps the reason why the Brahmins could not convert each salai into a caste category, (since it would then necessitate hierarchy) and instead assigned all of them the Kshatriya status.

In fact, this society does not seem to have a clear-cut hierarchy. We can distinguish different exclusive groups and communities, but cannot place them in a neat hierarchical set-up within the *salai* structure. All the *salais* have the same status, except the categories of Mks (Maharajkumars) and RKs (Rajkumars), whose higher status is marked by some additional rituals conducted during the marriage ceremonies and the special honorific terms addressed to them. The Brahmins are also entitled to specific respectful terms. Hence the Society comprises of Meiteis, Brahmins, Muslims, Lois, the hill people and mayangs. All these communities can be categorized as 'separate but equal'. Whatever the differential status or prejudices and biases that were observed they were not of an ascribed nature but generally rooted in historical events. The prejudice against the Lois was because they had refused to become Hindu and were consequently declared outcasts by the kind. And the prejudice against the Mayangs was because they had settled in Manipur without incorporating the indigenous culture. Lastly, the Hinduism of the Meiteis did not bind them to the Hindu communities outside Manipur and nor to the ones living in Manipur, since the Meitei brand of Vaishnava Hinduism existed exclusively in the domain of religion, while Hinduism as practised by the rest of Indian society, was intrinsically enmeshed in the entire social structure. The Meiteis can, therefore, be considered a Hindu society, if one looks at the overt symbols of their festivities, and yet believers of their own 'Meitei' faith, if the covert gestures of their faith are analyzed.

The Rites and the Rituals

The Rites and the Rituals was the area where Hinduism, or more precisely Vaishnava Hinduism, had the greatest influence. It succeeded in diluting, and some times, even disintegrating, the rites and rituals pertaining to the traditional Meitei faith. A few new Hindu rites and rituals were also adopted and incorporated. Yet, in the event of bringing a child to this world, and sending the soul of the being back to heaven, the required rituals were and still are conducted by the maibas and the maibis. All the other intermediate rites-of-passage were influenced by Hinduism, which nevertheless retained some of the traditional cultural characteristics. With new elements incorporated and old elements modified, the rites and rituals pertaining to this society evolved as 'Meitei Hindu rituals', rather than just as Hindu rituals. We shall see how the Meitei brand of Hinduism is distinctly different from the rites and rituals of the Hindus in the rest of India.

Societal norms, prior to the advent of Hinduism were not conducive to the formation of a full-fledged Hindu state. The caste system, the concept of purity- impurity, untouchability, hierarchy, ascribed division of labour, etc., which form important bases for the establishment of the tenets of Hinduism, were (and to some extent still are) absent in the Meitei social structure. Hinduism had to be initially imposed on the Meitei people by making it a state religion. But it could only put a blanket of Hindu festivals and rituals over the Meitei beliefs, rites, and beneath which the system of the traditional faith retained its roots. Scholars, pundits, and intelligentsia of that time, and even of present times, tried and are still trying to draw a parallel between Hindu and Meitei gods and rituals, to the extent that they attempted to derive an evolutionary line from *Indra* such that, for some Atiya Sidaba[8] became just another name for *Indra*[9]. The names of the *salais* became Brahmin *gotras* and Vishnu became the ancestor of all royal descendants, replacing Pakhangba. Nongpok Ningthou became Shiva and Panthoibi (the divine light) became Parvati and Durga simultaneously.

The practice of burning fire (*Phunga-Apokpa)* inside the house was traced to Vedic antiquity.

As already mentioned, all these newly introduced festivals and rituals, could only be formal signs of Hinduism and could never interfere entirely with the Meitei belief in their own ancestors. This is not to say that Hinduism did not influence the Meiteis. Some scholars and some sections of the people, who were deeply persuaded by the doctrine of Vaishnavism became staunch Hindus and were devout devotees of Krishna. In talking to them I realized that the idea that influenced them most strongly was their notion of Vaishnava Hinduism as a 'higher' and 'civilized' religious doctrine through which they could become part of the 'high' Sanskritic tradition of pan-Hindu India. They were also convinced that *Lai-haraoba*, Pakhangba, the directional deities etc., formed the 'lower' strata in religious philosophies, since they belonged to an 'animistic' form of worship as the category of ancestor cult, which was way down in the evolutionary theory of religions of the world and hence linked to primitive stages of societal development.

These people formulated another theory to justify the constituent elements of Meitei beliefs and practices, by describing them as 'tantrik' practices, including them in the fold of Hinduism, although much lower in the hierarchy, as part of the pan-Hindu, although much lower in the hierarchy, as part of the pan-Hindu ideology.

Except for the areas of Phayeng, Andro, Sekmai etc., Meiteis in other areas got converted to Vaishnavism during the reign of Garibniwaz, though there are a few households in the outskirts of Imphal, which have been practising Meitei religion since times immemorial.

According to one *Ima guru* (learned mother) no one in the interior was spared from forcible conversion to Hinduism. It was only about fifty years ago that revivalism was allowed to emerge in the interiors.

During the reign of Churachand Maharaj[10] all those who tried to follow the old religion openly were persecuted; many were jailed. Those Hindu Meitei who invited any one adhering to the old religion used to be ostracized by society. It was only during the reign of Bodhachandra Maharaj that the Meiteis were able to practice their old religion unhindered. The woman in Khongman explained this liberal outlook by saying that Bodhachandra had the 'real' royal blood of Pakhangba.

Though Meitei religion was observed during the reign of Garibaniwaz, Bhagyachandra, and Churachand, it was never observed publicly. Every household had special places for the *lainingthou, Leimaren* and the *Phunga Apokpa,* even though Garibniwaz had announced the threat of death if such places were maintained in the households.

During those times, some old people told me that the Meiteis used to worship these deities secretly at night in order to avoid persecution by the king. The leftover of the offering to the *'Apokpa'* was buried inside the residential area so that neighbors could not witness it or inform the king, who was sure to punish such persons.

After embracing Vaishnavism, King Pamheiba decided that the Brahmins became the conductors of rituals connected with the birth, marriage and death. In other words the Brahmins became the officiating priest in guiding each person's life cycle ritual. The role of the Maibas and the Maibis though lessened, yet could not be diminished. It is still a maibi who cuts the umbilical chord. No Meitei marriage is complete without seeking blessings of the three Apokpas; Atiya Sidaba, Sanamahi, and Pakhangba. And it is only after the maiba has declared the person officially dead that that the Brahmins can take over.

The Public Rituals

Without any confrontation, the Meiteis celebrate the Hindu festivals related of Krishna, with as much devotion as they celebrate their own traditional festivals. An exception consists of those Meiteis, who do not like to attend their own traditional festival, believing them to be remnants of the primitive stage of their society, and who regard themselves, after having become Hindus, as having reached a 'more civilized' State. There are also some revivalists of the Meitei cult who do not celebrate Hindu festivals. Hindu festivals are celebrated with utmost sincerity and devotion but an element of gaiety, and festivity, which is associated with the celebration of traditional Meitei festivals, seems to be toned down while celebrating Hindu festivals. There is usually an atmosphere of formality, awe, seriousness and subdued behaviors. While in the festival of the Meitei faith, there is spontaneity, gaiety, and informality and enjoyment.

From Meitei to Hindu Rituals: The Shift of Power

As stated before, when Hinduism was declared a state religion the king banned the practice of traditional beliefs and rituals, and gave patronage to the festivals revolving around the Vaishnava cult of Hinduism. People seen practicing traditional ritual were put to death and a large number who did not agree to get converted were ex-communicated. In spite of such restrictions the Meiteis even at the height of Vaishnavism continued to practice their own religion, in secrecy earlier and openly later on.

The 'Hindu' kings extended their patronage to Hindu festivities. Festivals like *yaoshang (Holi), Kang jatra (Rath Yara),* and *Janmashtami* are even today testimony to the patronage they got earlier. First of all, these festivals center around the Gobindajee and Vijay Gobinda temples, which are still under the care of the MKs and the RKs, and are important signifiers of the establishment of Hinduism in the state. Court ceremonialism extends to these political establishments. People follow the Hindu rituals as directed, and most of the time remain mere overt participants. In spite of the fact that state patronage was taken away and the elaborate and exuberant official arrangements were eliminated, the traditional festivals remain and continue as 'unofficial' private festivals. But this patronage could be extended only to the performative aspects, i.e., the ritual celebrations, for when it came to the belief system, no amount of state power could change the way the Meitei mind wanted to perceive its cosmic world.

It can be said that while Hindu Philosophy and the Hindu belief system had influenced the indigenous belief system it has not supplanted it.

With such a deeply ingrained belief system where every part of the human body and the state is considered to be the abode of gods, it is no wonder that the conversion to Hinduism did not erase the already existing faith. In fact, in spite of state patronage, Hinduism, in order to establish itself in the society, had to accept the prevalent ethnic elements and modify itself to such an extent, that it became a 'Meitei brand of Hinduism'.

The various claims made by sociologists in their theories on Hinduism in India do not cover the form of Hinduism practised in Manipur. The theoretical paradigm underlining Homo-Heirarchicus fails to establish its universal applicability in the light of the structure of Manipur Hinduism.

In fact Manipur Hinduism should be studied in greater details to throw more light on the extent to which a religion can undergo reformulations and remodeling in order to be accepted in a new social setting. It was one of the rare occasions in the history of Hinduism where it succeeded in bringing about mass conversion. A deeper understanding of this could bring out some more useful insights, which would make Dumont's Homo-Hierarchicus obsolete. It was Hinduism with no caste-system, no concept of ingrained purity-impurity and no ascribed division of labour. We have yet to come across a sociological study of Hinduism where these categories do not form part of any analysis.

NOTES

1. This paper is based on the book by the author titled, *Politics, Society and Cosmology in India's North East*, OUP, 1998.
2. A.M.Hocart, in *Kings and Councillors: An Essay in the Comparative Anatomy of Human Society*, (ed.) Rodhney Needham, University of Chicago Press, 1970, xxvii-xxviii
3. *ibid*, p. 35.
4. *ibid*, p. 37.
5. Clifford Geertz, Negara, p.124.
6. L. Dumont, *Homo-Hierarchicus: The Caste System and its Implications*, University of Chicago Press, Chicago, 1980.
7. M. Weber, *The Religion of India*, Hans H. Gerth and Don Martindale, The Free Press, New York, 1958.

8. The sky god in Meitei belief.
9. The Lord of Heaven in the Hindu Pantheon.
10. The first king installed by the British when Manipur was under their rule.

REFERENCES

Dumont, L. *Homo Hierarchicus: The Caste System and its Implications*, Chicago University Press, Chicago, 1980.

Evans Pritchard, EE. *Witchcraft, Oracles, and Magic among the Azande*, Clarendon Press, Oxford, 1937.

Geertz, Clifford. *The Interpretation of Cultures: Selected Essays*, Basic Books Inc., Publishers, New York, 1973.

Geertz, Clifford. *Negara: The Theatre State in 19th Century Bali,* Princeton University Press, Princeton, 1980.

Geertz, Clifford. *Works and Lives: The Anthropologist as an Author*. Polity Press, Cambridge, 1988.

Hocart, AM. *Caste: A Comparative Study,* Methuen Co. Ltd., London, 1950.

Hocart, AM. *The Life Giving Myth and Other Essays*, Lord Raglan (ed) Tavistok Publications (n.d.).

Hocart, AM. *Kings and Councillors: An Essay in the Comparative Anatomy of Human Society*, Rodhney Needham (ed), The University of Chicago Press, Chicago, 1970.

Index

❑❑❑